MOHANDAS
GANDHI

Spiritual Leaders and Thinkers

MARY BAKER EDDY

MOHANDAS GANDHI

AYATOLLAH RUHOLLAH KHOMEINI

MARTIN LUTHER

AIMEE SEMPLE McPHERSON

THOMAS MERTON

DALAI LAMA (TENZIN GYATSO)

SPIRITUAL
LEADERS AND
THINKERS

MOHANDAS GANDHI

Anne M. Todd

Introductory Essay by
Martin E. Marty, Professor Emeritus
University of Chicago Divinity School

CHELSEA HOUSE
PUBLISHERS

A Haights Cross Communications Company

Philadelphia

CHELSEA HOUSE PUBLISHERS

VP, NEW PRODUCT DEVELOPMENT   Sally Cheney
DIRECTOR OF PRODUCTION   Kim Shinners
CREATIVE MANAGER   Takeshi Takahashi
MANUFACTURING MANAGER   Diann Grasse

Staff for MOHANDAS GANDHI

EXECUTIVE EDITOR   Lee Marcott
SENIOR EDITOR   Tara Koellhoffer
PRODUCTION EDITOR   Megan Emery
ASSISTANT PHOTO EDITOR   Noelle Nardone
SERIES AND COVER DESIGNER   Keith Trego
LAYOUT   21st Century Publishing and Communications, Inc.

A Haights Cross Communications ◀▌ Company

www.chelseahouse.com

First Printing

9 8 7 6 5 4 3 2 1

Library of Congress Cataloging-in-Publication Data

Todd, Anne M.
  Mohandas Gandhi / by Anne M. Todd.
    p. cm. — (Spiritual leaders and thinkers)
  Includes bibliographical references and index.
  ISBN 0-7910-7864-7
  1. Gandhi, Mahatma, 1869-1948—Juvenile literature. 2. Nationalists—
India—Biography—Juvenile literature. 3. Statesmen—India—Biography—
Juvenile literature. [1. Gandhi, Mahatma, 1869-1948. 2. Statesmen. 3.
India—Politics and government—1919-1947.] I. Title. II. Series.
  DS481.G3T59 2004
  954.03'5'092—dc22

                                                        2003028105

CONTENTS

Foreword

Why become acquainted with notable people when making efforts to understand the religions of the world?

Most of the faith communities number hundreds of millions of people. What can attention paid to one tell about more, if not most, to say nothing of *all*, their adherents? Here is why:

The people in this series are exemplars. If you permit me to take a little detour through medieval dictionaries, their role will become clear.

In medieval lexicons, the word *exemplum* regularly showed up with a peculiar definition. No one needs to know Latin to see that it relates to "example" and "exemplary." But back then, *exemplum* could mean something very special.

That "ex-" at the beginning of such words signals "taking out" or "cutting out" something or other. Think of to "excise" something, which is to snip it out. So, in the more interesting dictionaries, an *exemplum* was referred to as "a clearing in the woods," something cut out of the forests.

These religious figures are *exempla*, figurative clearings in the woods of life. These clearings and these people perform three functions:

First, they define. You can be lost in the darkness, walking under the leafy canopy, above the undergrowth, plotless in the pathless forest. Then you come to a clearing. It defines with a sharp line: there, the woods end; here, the open space begins.

Great religious figures are often stumblers in the dark woods.

We see them emerging in the bright light of the clearing, blinking, admitting that they had often been lost in the mysteries of existence, tangled up with the questions that plague us all, wandering without definition. Then they discover the clearing, and, having done so, they point our way to it. We then learn more of who we are and where we are. Then we can set our own direction.

Second, the *exemplum*, the clearing in the woods of life, makes possible a brighter vision. Great religious pioneers in every case experience illumination and then they reflect their light into the hearts and minds of others. In Buddhism, a key word is *enlightenment*. In the Bible, "the people who walked in darkness have seen a great light." They see it because their prophets or savior brought them to the sun in the clearing.

Finally, when you picture a clearing in the woods, an *exemplum*, you are likely to see it as a place of cultivation. Whether in the Black Forest of Germany, on the American frontier, or in the rain forests of Brazil, the clearing is the place where, with light and civilization, residents can cultivate, can produce culture. As an American moviegoer, my mind's eye remembers cinematic scenes of frontier days and places that pioneers hacked out of the woods. There, they removed stones, planted, built a cabin, made love and produced families, smoked their meat, hung out laundered clothes, and read books. All that can happen in clearings.

In the case of these religious figures, planting and cultivating and harvesting are tasks in which they set an example and then inspire or ask us to follow. Most of us would not have the faintest idea how to find or be found by God, to nurture the Holy Spirit, to create a philosophy of life without guidance. It is not likely that most of us would be satisfied with our search if we only consulted books of dogma or philosophy, though such may come to have their place in the clearing.

Philosopher Søren Kierkegaard properly pointed out that you cannot learn to swim by being suspended from the ceiling on a belt and reading a "How To" book on swimming. You learn because a parent or an instructor plunges you into water, supports you when necessary, teaches you breathing and motion, and then releases you to swim on your own.

Kierkegaard was not criticizing the use of books. I certainly have nothing against books. If I did, I would not be commending this series to you, as I am doing here. For guidance and courage in the spiritual quest, or—and this is by no means unimportant!—in intellectual pursuits, involving efforts to understand the paths others have taken, there seems to be no better way than to follow a fellow mortal, but a man or woman of genius, depth, and daring. We "see" them through books like these.

Exemplars come in very different styles and forms. They bring differing kinds of illumination, and then suggest or describe diverse patterns of action to those who join them. In the case of the present series, it is possible for someone to repudiate or disagree with *all* the religious leaders in this series. It is possible also to be nonreligious and antireligious and therefore to disregard the truth claims of all of them. It is more difficult, however, to ignore them. Atheists, agnostics, adherents, believers, and fanatics alike live in cultures that are different for the presence of these people. "Leaders and thinkers" they may be, but most of us do best to appraise their thought in the context of the lives they lead or have led.

If it is possible to reject them all, it is impossible to affirm everything that all of them were about. They disagree with each other, often in basic ways. Sometimes they develop their positions and ways of thinking by separating themselves from all the others. If they met each other, they would likely judge each other cruelly. Yet the lives of each and all of them make a contribution to the intellectual and spiritual quests of those who go in ways other than theirs. There are tens of thousands of religions in the world, and millions of faith communities. Every one of them has been shaped by founders and interpreters, agents of change and prophets of doom or promise. It may seem arbitrary to walk down a bookshelf and let a finger fall on one or another, almost accidentally. This series may certainly look arbitrary in this way. Why precisely the choice of these exemplars?

In some cases, it is clear that the publishers have chosen someone who has a constituency. Many of the world's 54 million Lutherans may be curious about where they got their name, who the man Martin Luther was. Others are members of a community but choose isolation: The hermit monk Thomas Merton is typical. Still others are exiled and achieve their work far from the clearing in which they grew up; here the Dalai Lama is representative. Quite a number of the selected leaders had been made unwelcome, or felt unwelcome in the clearings, in their own childhoods and youth. This reality has almost always been the case with women like Mary Baker Eddy or Aimee Semple McPherson. Some are extremely controversial: Ayatollah Ruhollah Khomeini stands out. Yet to read of this life and thought as one can in this series will be illuminating in much of the world of conflict today.

Reading of religious leaders can be a defensive act: Study the lives of certain ones among them and you can ward off spiritual— and sometimes even militant—assaults by people who follow them. Reading and learning can be a personally positive act: Most of these figures led lives that we can indeed call exemplary. Such lives can throw light on communities of people who are in no way tempted to follow them. I am not likely to be drawn to the hermit life, will not give up my allegiance to medical doctors, or be successfully nonviolent. Yet Thomas Merton reaches me and many non-Catholics in our communities; Mary Baker Eddy reminds others that there are more ways than one to approach healing; Mohandas Gandhi stings the conscience of people in cultures like ours where resorting to violence is too frequent, too easy.

Finally, reading these lives tells something about how history is made by imperfect beings. None of these subjects is a god, though some of them claimed that they had special access to the divine, or that they were like windows that provided for illumination to that which is eternal. Most of their stories began with inauspicious childhoods. Sometimes they were victimized, by parents or by leaders of religions from which they later broke.

Some of them were unpleasant and abrasive. They could be ungracious toward those who were near them and impatient with laggards. If their lives were symbolic clearings, places for light, many of them also knew clouds and shadows and the fall of night. How they met the challenges of life and led others to face them is central to the plot of all of them.

I have often used a rather unexciting concept to describe what I look for in books: *interestingness.* The authors of these books, one might say, had it easy, because the characters they treat are themselves so interesting. But the authors also had to be interesting and responsible. If, as they wrote, they would have dulled the personalities of their bright characters, that would have been a flaw as marring as if they had treated their subjects without combining fairness and criticism, affection and distance. To my eye, and I hope in yours, they take us to spiritual and intellectual clearings that are so needed in our dark times.

Martin E. Marty
The University of Chicago

1

March to the Sea

If my letter makes no appeal to your heart, on the eleventh day of this month I shall proceed with such co-workers of the Ashram as I can take, to disregard the provisions of the Salt Laws. I regard this tax to be the most iniquitous of all from the poor man's standpoint. As the Independence movement is essentially for the poorest in the land, the beginning will be made with this evil.

—Gandhi in a letter to
the British viceroy for India

Around 6:30 A.M. on March 12, 1930, a thin, scantily clad, nearly bald man of sixty years stepped onto the road leading away from his home. He lived in Ahmedabad, located in northwestern India. In one hand, he carried a long walking stick. He was dressed in simple clothes made out of a coarse, hand-woven material called *khadi*. He wore a *dhoti*, or a kind of loincloth similar to baggy shorts; a shawl draped over his shoulders; and wooden sandals. When he smiled, one could see that he was missing numerous teeth. He wore small, steel-rimmed glasses. Yet for a seemingly frail man, his steps were sure and strong. This man was anything but frail. He was Mohandas Karamchand Gandhi, known as the *Mahatma*, or "Great Soul."

Behind Gandhi walked seventy-eight men and women. They were all headed south toward Dandi, a city located on the west coast of India, on the Arabian Sea. The journey totaled 241 miles. It would take the group twenty-four days to walk. They walked during the coolest parts of the day—the early morning and late evening. At night, the walkers slept outside, under the shelter of trees. During the middle of the day, Gandhi stopped in villages and spoke to the residents, urging them to join his cause.

Gandhi's reason for undertaking this journey was to protest the taxing of Indian salt, one of India's natural resources. In 1930, the British Empire ruled India. The British, as well as the French, had first come to India in the 1700s. At that time, Great Britain and France took control of much of India. Gradually, the British pushed out the French until India was turned into a British colony in 1858.

The British did not treat the Indians well. Under British law, Indians were not allowed to collect or make their own salt, which continually washed up from the sea onto their coastal shores. Not only did the Indians have to buy the processed salt they needed from the British, but they also had to pay a tax on that salt. To call attention to the injustice of the salt laws, Gandhi planned to publicly break the law by gathering salt himself.

Thousands of Indians joined Gandhi and his followers as they made their way to the coast. On April 5, the marchers arrived at Dandi. That evening and the following morning, Gandhi and the other demonstrators prayed at the edge of the sea. Then, at exactly 6:00 A.M., he and his followers walked into the sea for their morning bath, a traditional Hindu custom. Following the bath, Gandhi returned to the shore, bent over, and took a pinch of raw salt from the sand. At that moment, Gandhi broke the law.

An article that appeared in an Indian newspaper shortly after the demonstration said,

> The scenes that preceded, accompanied and followed this great national event were so enthusiastic, magnificent and soul-stirring that indeed they beggar description. Never was the wave of patriotism so powerful in the hearts of mankind, as it was on this great occasion which is bound to go down to the chapters of the history of India's national freedom as a great beginning of a Great Movement . . . [1]

Eleven months later, on March 5, 1931, the British government agreed to allow those Indians living along the coast to make their own salt.

In fighting for his cause, Gandhi had not drawn a gun or used threats to express his views. He had not burned down a building or beaten up a government official. He had used civil disobedience, or nonviolent refusal to obey a law perceived as unjust. Gandhi believed that people could peacefully—through the force of truth and love—obtain the political and social changes they wanted. He once described his reasoning for using a campaign of civil disobedience against the British. He said, "The British . . . want us to put the struggle on the plane of machine guns where they have the weapons and we do not. Our only assurance of beating them is putting the struggle on a plane where we have the weapons and they do not." [2]

Albert Einstein said of Gandhi, "Generations to come will scarce believe that such a one as this ever in flesh and blood walked upon this earth." [3] From 1920 to 1947, Gandhi went on frequent fasts, or periods of not eating; led boycotts against the purchase of British goods; met with villagers to encourage simple living and self-reliance; and organized peaceful protests against the British. His actions held a common purpose: to correct injustices against Indians and to bring independence to India. How did Mohandas Gandhi, this seemingly small, weak man, come to face such enormous challenges? What obstacles did he meet along the way? Was Gandhi ever able to discover what he sought all his life: truth and love?

2

Growing up in India

The real property that a parent can transmit to all equally is his or her character and educational facilities.

—Mohandas Gandhi

On October 2, 1869, in the town of Porbandar, India, Putlibai Gandhi gave birth to a son. This was Putlibai's fourth and last child. She and her husband, Karamchand (called Kaba), named their son Mohandas Karamchand Gandhi, or "Mohan" for short. Kaba and Putlibai now had four children together: one daughter, Raliatbehn (the oldest of their children, born in 1862), and three sons—Laxmidas, born in 1863; Karsandas, born in 1866; and Mohandas, born in 1869.

Prior to marrying Putlibai, Kaba had been married three times and had fathered a daughter with each of his first two wives. His third wife had not been able to have children. All three of Kaba's previous wives had died. When Kaba married Putlibai, he was nearly forty years old; Putlibai was only thirteen.

Kaba, Putlibai, their four children, and Kaba's two daughters from his previous marriages lived in a many-roomed, three-story house in Porbandar. The city of Porbandar is located on the Kathiawar Peninsula, on the western side of India next to the Arabian Sea. The streets were narrow and crowded with bazaars. Most of the city was constructed from limestone, which, over time, had turned white. The whitened buildings of Porbandar won it the nickname "White City."

The house in which the Gandhis lived had been in the family since 1777, when it was bought by Mohandas's great-grandfather. It was in this house, with the help of a midwife, that Mohandas Gandhi was born.

Most of the rooms were small. The few windows were also small, leaving the whole house with little light and poor circulation. But the house was not lacking bustle and activity. Sharing the Gandhi household were Kaba's five brothers, their families, and numerous servants, making for a total of somewhere between twenty and twenty-five people living together. This arrangement was a common practice in India, where many people lived with their extended families.

PUTLIBAI GANDHI

Putlibai Gandhi was a loving mother. In fact, she treated all of the children living in the Gandhi house as if they were her own. She had a close relationship with her youngest child, Mohan. She held high expectations for him, seeing something in Mohan that

HINDUISM

Mohandas and his family, like the majority of Indians, were Hindu. A smaller, but still sizable, number of Indians were Muslim. Hinduism is an ancient religion that predates recorded history; it is the oldest religion in the world. There is no known founder of Hinduism.

Religion was the center of Gandhi's family life. Hinduism affected what they ate, how they dressed, how they treated others, who they married, and how they defined their value system. There are numerous Hindu sects, such as Shaivism, Shaktism, and Vaishnavism. Each sect honors different gods and has different beliefs. The Gandhi family belonged to the Vaishnavist sect.

Hinduism's tolerance for worshiping different gods sets it apart from most other religions. Some Hindus worship Vishnu (the Preserver god), others Brahma (the Creator god), and still others Shiva (the Destroyer god). Hindus accept other religions, including Christianity, Judaism, and Buddhism, without feelings of superiority. This tolerance is obtainable because Hindus believe that all religions lead to finding truth for the soul. How each soul finds that truth (and to what god a person prays in order to find it) is not as important as reaching the truth.

Part of the Hindu social structure includes the caste system, common to all Hindu sects. Hindus are divided into different castes: first, the Brahmins, or priests; second, the Kshatriyas, or princes and soldiers; third, the Vaishyas, or merchants and farmers; and fourth, the Shudras, or laborers and peasants. People were born into a particular caste, taking on the same caste as their parents. If you were born a Shudra, for example, you had no way of eventually becoming a Vaishya. The Gandhis were a part of the third-ranking Vaishya caste. The name "Gandhi" means "grocer," although Mohandas's father and grand-fathers had been politicians, not grocers.

The rest of the people, which included about 70 million Hindus who did not fit into one of the above castes, were called the Untouchables. The Untouchables lived in extreme poverty and faced much discrimination. If a person from an upper caste came upon an Untouchable, the upper-caste person would likely cross the street to avoid being contaminated.

she did not see in her other children. She said extra prayers for Mohan and gave him special attention. In return, Mohan looked up to her and respected her.

Putlibai was deeply religious. Each day, she took Mohan and the rest of her children to the Vaishnava Hindu temple, located conveniently next door to the Gandhi house, to pray and honor the Hindu gods. Putlibai also took her children along with her when she tended to the lower castes and helped nurse the sick. From her actions, Mohan learned to show respect, kindness, and love to all people.

Putlibai also held a great interest in learning about world events. Women throughout Porbandar respected and admired Putlibai for her knowledge and intelligence and came to her with questions and requests for advice. Mohan, too, greatly respected his mother's intelligence and desire to learn.

KARAMCHAND GANDHI

Karamchand Gandhi was a political figure in Porbandar. Like his father, Uttamchand Gandhi, Karamchand had become a court official, or chief minister, of the local ruling prince of Porbandar. Karamchand's duties included advising the royal family of Porbandar and hiring other government officials.

Mohan did not see a great deal of his father during his childhood, as Karamchand was often away from home—sometimes for months at a time—with his work. Mohandas later described his father as "truthful, brave and generous, but short-tempered."[4] It is customary for Hindu fathers not to shower their sons with too much affection. As a result, Mohan's father sometimes came across as aloof and overly strict.

Karamchand did not have a formal education. He learned from experience by watching his father work and attending religious ceremonies. There were some areas, however, in which he never gained much knowledge, including geography and history. Nonetheless, Karamchand excelled as chief minister in Porbandar.

In spite of Karamchand's success in his job, he did not find ways to accumulate wealth. The Gandhis had plenty to eat, a respectable number of servants, and a few nice pieces of furniture, but they were by no means wealthy. The money Karamchand brought in just covered the household expenses.

MOHAN'S CHILDHOOD

Mohandas was a shy boy with few friends. He usually kept to himself, coming directly home from school each day and avoiding his classmates, most of whom were taller, heavier, and more outgoing than he was. Mohan was scared of the dark, and of ghosts and spirits. He made sure to light his room at night so as not to be in complete darkness. Still, his fears haunted him. He turned to his nurse for help. His nurse, named Rambha, doted on Mohan endlessly and offered him a cure for his fears: to repeat the word *Ramanama*, a Hindu god. Mohan used this advice and took comfort from it later in life under a variety of circumstances.

Although Mohan was quiet among his classmates, he was lively and active at home. He enjoyed playing with dogs and teasing his sister, Raliatbehn, who was often given the task of watching over her younger brother. Though keeping track of one boy may not sound difficult, Mohan proved to be a handful, often getting into mischief. When he was in a more solitary mood, Mohan spent his time caring for plants, which was a favorite pastime for him.

GOING TO SCHOOL

Mohandas did not do well at Dhooli Shala, the primary school he attended in Porbandar. There, he and the other students learned to write letters by tracing them in dust. Mohan found it difficult to memorize the required material, such as multiplication tables, and he took little interest in trying to excel.

Mohan also did not feel he fit in with the other students at Dhooli Shala. The boys would join together in reciting mean rhymes about the teacher. Mohan did not see the point in such actions and remained quiet. When the other boys roughhoused on the playground, Mohan would stand on the sidelines, with no desire to join in the games.

Although Mohandas was different from the other boys, he had a strong sense of self, even at a very young age. As a result, he was not disturbed or bothered by being different; he accepted it as a part of who he was. Like his mother, Mohan held high morals and, above all else, sought truth. In addition, he was deeply devoted to his parents and strove to make them proud. His drive to be "good" would help guide him through his childhood, as he encountered peer pressures and temptations to experiment with non-Hindu ways.

In 1876, a year after beginning school at Dhooli Shala, Mohan and his family moved to the city of Rajkot, located 120 miles east of Porbandar. Mohan's father had taken a new job as the *diwan*, or chief administrator, of the principality of Rajkot. It was Karamchand's job to settle problems among the town's people.

Rajkot offered an education superior to that found in Porbandar. Still, Mohandas struggled with his studies and remained a mediocre student. After finishing primary school, Mohandas entered Alfred Boys High School when he turned twelve. Mohandas's two older brothers attended the high school at the same time. Here, Mohandas had his first introduction to the English language, which he found difficult to learn.

He did become inspired by two plays he read outside of the classroom, however. Until this time, Mohandas had not had any desire to read beyond what was required of him through school. But these plays caught his attention and changed his attitude about reading. One was *Shravana Pitribhakti Nataka*; the other, *Harishchandra*. The first was about Shravana, a boy completely devoted to his blind parents. To show his devotion, Shravana even carried his parents in baskets balanced on his shoulders. The second play was about how the lead character, Harishchandra, managed to stay truthful through many ordeals. Both plays greatly influenced Mohandas, inspiring him to live his life as these characters had done.

EARLY MARRIAGE

One year after entering Alfred Boys High School, Mohandas was still adjusting to the new place and his new studies. He had a lot going on in his life. Yet at the young age of thirteen, he found himself faced with a huge life change. Mohan was getting married.

Mohandas had not chosen his bride; instead, the marriage had been arranged by the two families. Mohandas's bride was Kasturbai Makanji, also thirteen years old. She was petite and pretty at the time of their wedding, and she grew up to be an even more beautiful woman. Kasturbai had grown up in Porbandar, just a few blocks from the Gandhi household. Her father, a close friend of Karamchand's, was a wealthy merchant and the family lived well.

The wedding was an elaborate affair that included not just Mohandas and Kasturbai's marriage, but two others on the same day as well—the wedding of Mohandas's older brother, Karsandas, and the wedding of a cousin. The triple wedding was given months of thought and preparation. Mohandas knew nothing of the wedding until it was already in the planning stages. He later said, "It was only through these preparations that we got warning of the coming event. I do not think it meant to me anything more than the prospect of good clothes to wear, drum beating, marriage processions, rich dinners and a strange girl to play with." [5]

The ceremony included *Saptapadi*, a Hindu wedding custom. During Saptapadi, the bride and groom take seven steps together while making promises of devotion and fidelity. Following the ceremony, the two inexperienced thirteen-year-olds spent their first night together as husband and wife.

After the wedding took place, Kasturbai and Mohandas lived with Mohandas's parents. During the first few years of their marriage, Kasturbai would leave for a few months at a time to stay with her parents, which was customary in such child-marriages. Mohandas learned quickly that having a successful marriage required traits that he did not yet possess—especially trust.

Over the years, Mohandas and Kasturbai came to love, respect, support, and trust one another, so much so that they remained together for sixty-two years. These were not feelings and behaviors that came immediately, however. In the early years of their marriage, they faced numerous challenges. Mohandas felt an intense passion for his young, beautiful new wife. Along with that passion came a feeling of possession and nagging jealousy. Mohandas forbade his wife to leave the house without his permission, but Kasturbai had a mind of her own. She was not going to be housebound and she refused to be told what to do. She came and went as she pleased, much to Mohandas's disapproval. As a result, the couple would bicker and then spend hours not speaking to each other.

Mohandas also became increasingly lustful of his new bride. He focused all of his energy on being with Kasturbai. At school, he spent the day watching the clock, waiting to get home to be with his wife once again. As a result, his grades dropped and his feelings of jealousy increased.

In addition, Mohandas was disturbed by the fact that Kasturbai was illiterate. He wanted her to learn to read and write, but she showed little or no desire to do so. Mohandas's early attempts to teach Kasturbai to read and write had little success and left him frustrated.

Perhaps what saved the marriage was the time Mohandas and Kasturbai spent apart, when she would leave him to live with her parents for a while. During the time away from each other, they could both put the relationship into perspective and reexamine their priorities and values. The young couple did share genuine positive feelings for one another, which were able to surface and, over the years, eventually calmed Mohandas's possessive and jealous feelings and turned them into love and trust.

3

Leaving Home for College

All your scholarship would be in vain if at the same
time you do not build your character and attain
mastery over your thoughts and your actions.

—Mohandas Gandhi

Once married, Kasturbai and Mohandas Gandhi spent the next five years adjusting to their new lives. Although that first year after marriage was wasted for Gandhi at school, he did fare better than his brother, Karsandas, who had been married the same day. Karsandas was so wrapped up in his new marriage that he stopped going to school altogether. Gandhi, on the other hand, began to focus on his schoolwork as the novelty of his marriage wore off.

Gandhi's improvement in school was obvious when he brought home prizes and scholarships he had won for his academics. Gandhi was always surprised by these honors, however, because his studies did not come easily. Two subjects that proved to be especially difficult were geometry and Sanskrit, an ancient Hindu language. Luckily, Gandhi at last grasped an understanding of geometry and found that it was, in fact, easy—as well as interesting. Sanskrit was more difficult and Gandhi struggled throughout his years in school to master the language.

During his high school years, Gandhi experimented with something that would have greatly shocked his parents. One of Gandhi's friends, a Muslim boy named Sheikh Mehtab, convinced Gandhi that he should try eating meat. Hindus believe that cows are sacred and that a person should not kill a cow for its meat. Gandhi had never before tasted meat. Sheikh Mehtab told Gandhi that eating meat would make him stronger and claimed that if all Indians would eat meat, they would be able to defeat the British. Gandhi very much wanted to see India free from British rule. He decided to take Sheikh Mehtab's advice.

Eating meat meant that he would not only be going against the beliefs of his religion, but he would also be lying to his parents. This was something that Gandhi was not accustomed to doing. But for the good of his country and in the hope of making himself strong, Gandhi decided it had to be done. He first tried goat meat, which made him sick and gave him nightmares. Then, Sheikh Mehtab had fancy meat dishes prepared for him, which Gandhi grew to enjoy. Over the course of a year, he ate about six meat meals in total. But then Gandhi had a realization: Lying and deceiving his parents was worse than not eating meat. If he wanted to eat meat openly after his parents died, he could do so. Until then, he would abstain. Gandhi informed Sheikh Mehtab of his decision. He never ate meat again.

TRAGEDY STRIKES TWICE

While Gandhi was a teenager, his father became very sick with fistula, a disease in which an internal organ in the body leaks fluids. Over time, his condition worsened. For three years— from the time Gandhi was fourteen until he was sixteen— Karamchand was bedridden. He depended on the help of Putlibai, Gandhi, and a household servant to take care of him.

Mohandas Gandhi took his nursing duties very seriously. When he was not at school, he was taking care of his father. He left his father's room only to go on an evening walk, which he did only if his father permitted it or if his father was feeling unusually well. Otherwise, Gandhi was at his father's bedside, administrating his medicine or massaging his legs.

It was also at this time that Gandhi learned that his wife was pregnant with their first child. He felt ashamed because, to him, the pregnancy proved that he was unable to control the physical desire he felt for his wife, which, in turn, made him feel that his devotion to his parents had been clouded. Even so, Gandhi still rushed to his bedroom each night to be with his wife after having cared for his father.

Meanwhile, Karamchand was growing weaker. He saw numerous doctors and surgeons and tried many different medicines and treatments but nothing worked. Finally, an English surgeon told the family that Karamchand should have a surgical operation. The family physician disagreed. He felt that Karamchand was too old to go through with such a procedure. Putlibai and the rest of the family trusted the family physician's advice over the surgeon's and Gandhi's father did not receive the operation.

One of Karamchand's brothers was in town and came in on the evening of November 16, 1885, while Gandhi was caring for his father. His uncle offered to take over sitting with Karamchand and Gandhi readily agreed, eager to see his wife. While his uncle was filling in for Gandhi, Karamchand took his final breath.

Gandhi felt extremely guilty over his father's death. He had always prided himself on his devotion to his parents, yet in his father's final hours, Gandhi was not there for him. Gandhi felt he should have stayed with his father instead of accepting his uncle's offer to sit in for him.

Not long after his father's death, Kasturbai gave birth to their first child. The infant survived only a few days. Gandhi blamed himself. He felt that the death of the baby was the result of his own lustful feelings overpowering his devotion to his parents.

PREPARING FOR COLLEGE

At sixteen years old, Mohandas Gandhi had already faced the death of his father and his first child. Now he was about to graduate from high school and begin a new chapter in his life. In 1887, he took the matriculation examination, a test to enter college or a university, and passed. He decided to attend Samaldas College, located in Bhavnagar, about ninety miles from Rajkot. He left in January 1888. He did not do well academically or health-wise and returned home after just one term. Later that year, Gandhi and Kasturbai became the parents of their first surviving son, Harilal.

The Gandhi family called in an old friend and advisor, Mavji Dave, to discuss Gandhi's future. Mavji Dave said to Gandhi,

> . . . I want you to be Diwan, or if possible something better. Only in that way could you take under your protecting care your large family. The times are fast changing and getting harder every day. It is the wisest thing therefore to become a barrister. . . . When I come here next I shall expect to hear of preparations for England. Be sure to let me know if I can assist in any way.[6]

In this way, Gandhi was advised to attend a three-year law degree program in England. Gandhi liked the sound of it.

Putlibai was not pleased to hear that her youngest son was considering going to college in England. She had heard rumors that the young men there ate meat and drank liquor. She made Gandhi promise not to touch wine, meat, or women. Gandhi agreed. Satisfied, Putlibai gave her consent. Alfred Boys High School gave Gandhi a farewell party. In August 1888, Gandhi said good-bye to Kasturbai and their infant son, Harilal, and set off for Bombay, where he was to take a ship to England.

Others in the Rajkot community were not convinced that it was appropriate for Gandhi to travel to England. The members of the council in charge of the Vaishya caste, to which Gandhi belonged, met up with Gandhi in Bombay. They told Gandhi that it was against the Hindu religion to travel abroad, and they forbade him to leave India. Gandhi listened to their worries but held to his decision. He pointed out that he had permission from his family's advisor and from his mother and brothers. He told them about his promise not to eat meat, drink wine, or touch women. Gandhi was certain that his actions in England would not jeopardize his Hindu faith.

Nonetheless, the elders felt Gandhi should not travel to England. When Gandhi informed the elders that he planned to go anyway, they were outraged. The *sheth*, or headman of the community, said, "This boy shall be treated as an outcaste from today. Whoever helps him or goes to see him off at the dock shall be punishable with a fine of one rupee four annas."[7] From that day forward, Gandhi was shunned from his caste. Even upon Gandhi's return from England three years later, he did not attempt readmission.

Gandhi set sail for England from Bombay on September 4, 1888, aboard the S.S. *Clyde*. His roommate aboard the ship was Tryambakrai Mazmudar, who looked after Gandhi during his voyage. Mazmudar tried to persuade Gandhi to socialize with the other passengers, but Gandhi was shy and unwilling to converse in English, which did not come easily to him. Instead, Gandhi spent most of the voyage in his room, where he ate his meals and avoided the other passengers. At last, three and a half weeks after setting sail, the *Clyde* arrived at England's shore and Mohandas Gandhi began yet another chapter in his life.

COLLEGE LIFE

Once the ship landed, Gandhi went to London, where he lived for a short time in a hotel and then with an English family. Gandhi faced a number of challenges in London. First, he realized immediately that, while in India, he had purchased the wrong kind of clothes to wear in England. He had proudly left the ship wearing a new white flannel suit, but saw that English men wore dark suits, not light-colored suits. Once settled in his London room, he set out to remedy the problem and bought some dark-colored suits. Although Gandhi still looked like a foreigner, he felt like he stood out less among the English.

Another problem was the food. Gandhi was not very good at using forks and knives, which caused him to feel uncomfortable about eating in front of other people. He also had a hard time finding dishes that did not contain meat. During his first weeks in London, Gandhi ate very little, existing mostly on bread, jam, and fruit. His constant hunger added to his feelings of homesickness and Gandhi struggled with the desire to flee back to India. He held his ground, however, and remained in this strange, unfamiliar place. He had every intention of completing his three-year program.

Gandhi set to work making himself more comfortable in England. He read English newspapers and worked on his English-speaking skills until he felt less intimidated by the language. He walked the streets until he came upon a vegetarian restaurant located on Farringdon Street. This find was greatly uplifting to the ever-hungry Gandhi. He was at last able to eat a complete and filling meal. At the restaurant, he also purchased a book entitled *Plea for Vegetarianism*, written by Henry Stephens Salt. This book helped Gandhi clarify his true reasons for sticking to his vow. Although he had always told himself that he would take up eating meat after his parents had died, after reading the book, he realized he did not care to ever eat meat again. The decision to be a vegetarian was now his, not one made for his parents or for his religion. He joined the Vegetarian Society and was elected to its executive committee. Gandhi attended the meetings, though he was usually too shy to speak up.

Gandhi also began a flurry of lessons, which he hoped would make an English gentleman out of him. He briefly took French, violin, dancing, and elocution (public speaking) lessons. He did not excel at any of his classes and after a few months of struggling with them, Gandhi came to the realization that his stay in England was much too short to merit the effort. He stopped the classes and focused on his upcoming law classes.

During Gandhi's college years, he went about simplifying his life. He felt guilty about his brother's sending him money to live on, and wanted to make sure he was spending as little as possible. He moved out of the English family's home and rented two rooms; he later cut down to one room. He began to cook more and more of his meals in his room until he was eating only one meal a day at a restaurant. He also stopped taking public transportation and walked everywhere he needed to go. He could easily walk ten miles a day without strain or effort. These habits would stay with Gandhi for the rest of his years.

RETURNING HOME

On June 10, 1891, Mohandas Gandhi passed his examinations. Having been called to the bar, he was now officially a lawyer. Two days later, he set sail for India. He was going home. After a choppy voyage across the sea, during which Gandhi was one of the few passengers to avoid seasickness, Gandhi stepped onto Indian land once again. Meeting him at the dock was his brother Laxmidas.

Laxmidas and Mohandas stayed for a while with Laxmidas's friend Dr. P.J. Mehta and his brother. During their stay, Gandhi learned some devastating news: His mother had died while he was in England. Laxmidas had kept this from his brother, fearing that Gandhi would not be able to cope with

EXAMINING RELIGION

During his time in London, Gandhi learned about many religions. His college courses did not take up much of his time, so he spent a good deal of time exploring different belief systems, as well as his own. Although he had been raised a Hindu, he had not yet read the *Bhagavad Gita* (Song of the Lord). A sacred Hindu poem, the Bhagavad Gita was probably written about A.D. 100. In it, Krishna, an incarnation of the Hindu god Vishnu, talks to a prince about obtaining peace and teaches lessons about life and death. As a child, Gandhi's parents had read aloud excerpts from Bhagavad Gita to their children, but Gandhi had never read the poem in its entirety. Now he had the opportunity to do so in London, and he found it very inspiring. He ended up reading the text in its original Sanskrit, as well as nearly all of its translations.

One of Gandhi's favorite translations of Bhagavad Gita was that written by Sir Edwin Arnold. Arnold also wrote *The Light of Asia*, through which Gandhi learned much about Buddhism, a religion that has many similarities to Hinduism. The founder of Buddhism, Siddhartha Gautama, called simply the Buddha, believed that suffering came as a result of craving worldly things. This paralleled Gandhi's beliefs in living simply and avoiding excess. Unlike Hindus, Buddhists do not believe in the caste system. The Buddha believed that all people are equal and should be treated the same. Gandhi completely agreed with this philosophy and, throughout his life, he worked to rid India of its prejudice against Untouchables.

In addition to studying Hinduism and Buddhism, Gandhi studied Christianity. He read the Bible and, although he found little to admire in the Old Testament, he read the New Testament more carefully and compared some of its teachings to those in the Bhagavad Gita.

the loss while living in a foreign land away from his loved ones. Gandhi took the news hard, as his mother had been a great influence in his life and had instilled within him many of the life lessons that he would always treasure. He had looked up to his mother and respected her dearly. Gandhi kept his feelings of grief to himself, however, and did not show any signs of emotion to those around him. He went on with his life.

On his return to Rajkot, Gandhi discovered that although he had had a three-year separation from his wife, the young couple still struggled with the same problems they had experienced early in their marriage. Gandhi was often jealous and they were unable to communicate very effectively with each other. Their son Harilal was now almost four years old and was someone Gandhi hardly knew.

Gandhi did not have time to deal with his domestic problems, however. With encouragement from his brother Laxmidas, Gandhi decided to set up a law practice in Bombay. Before leaving for Bombay, Gandhi learned that Kasturbai was pregnant for a third time. Reluctantly leaving a pregnant Kasturbai and young Harilal once again, Gandhi temporarily moved to Bombay. He did not feel especially qualified to begin his own law practice, however. When he failed to make his case during his first trial experience, Gandhi returned his client's money, closed up his practice, and returned home to Rajkot.

Gandhi's second son, Manilal, was born in October 1892. Gandhi was happy at the time of his son's birth and hoped for more pleasant times for his family. Gandhi and Kasturbai's relationship—and their love for one another—began to grow stronger as time passed. Gandhi's feelings of jealousy and possession lessened as the bond between him and his wife grew. Work for Gandhi at this time was not exciting, but it was dependable. He was drawing up applications and memorials. He was making a respectable amount of money and the Gandhis were able to live comfortably.

In time, however, Gandhi realized that he wanted something more from his life. Then, Laxmidas heard of an opportunity for Gandhi to practice law in South Africa. Gandhi learned that the legal firm would pay his travel expenses and offer him a small fee for his services for one year. Gandhi felt ready to leave India and experience new surroundings once again. He decided to take the job.

4

Living in South Africa

*I should try, if possible, to root out the disease
[of colour prejudice] and suffer hardships in the process.
Redress for wrongs I should seek only to the
extent that would be necessary.*

—Mohandas Gandhi

For the third time, Gandhi found himself saying good-bye to his wife. This time, he was also leaving behind two children. It saddened Gandhi to leave his family, but he told them it would only be for one year.

Gandhi's new job would take him to the province of Natal, South Africa, where he would be working for Dada Abdulla, an Indian merchant in the ship trading business. Abdulla already had European lawyers representing him, but he wanted an Indian lawyer on his team to work as a clerk and to help with English translations.

Once again, Gandhi sailed from Bombay, India. He left on April 19, 1893, on a ship called *Safari*. He became good friends with the captain, who taught Gandhi how to play chess during their voyage. After several stops along the way, the ship reached the port of Durban in Natal near the end of May.

When Gandhi arrived in Natal, located on the coast of the Indian Ocean, he was completely unaware of the discrimination and hatred that the forty-three thousand Indians who lived there faced. That soon changed. He encountered his first taste of racism in a Durban court. He had arrived at the court with Dada Abdulla, who wanted to show Gandhi around and introduce him to some people. Upon getting seated and being introduced to those around him, Gandhi noticed that the magistrate kept looking at him. After a lengthy stare, the magistrate instructed Gandhi to remove his turban. Gandhi refused. Instead, he got up and left the courthouse.

Gandhi later learned from Abdulla that Indians, called "coolies" by the whites, were not allowed to wear turbans inside the courthouse. To an Indian, this was considered an insult, as the turban is a part of religious dress and culture. Rather than be insulted, Gandhi at first thought he would stop wearing a turban and wear an English hat instead. By doing this, he could spare himself insult. Abdulla disagreed with Gandhi's reasoning and told him, "If you do anything of the kind, it will have a very bad effect. You will compromise those insisting on wearing Indian turbans."[8] This advice seemed sound to Gandhi, who then decided to write to the local newspapers, explaining what had happened to him and defending his choice to wear a turban in court. The newspaper described Mohandas Gandhi as an "unwelcome visitor." Within just a few days of arriving in Natal, Gandhi had both made enemies and won supporters for his views.

Not long after this incident, Gandhi experienced a much more extreme encounter with racism. This incident would change the course of his entire stay in South Africa.

TRAVELING TO PRETORIA

Abdulla informed Gandhi that he was to travel to Pretoria to make preparations for a case. Gandhi agreed and boarded a train in Natal with a first-class ticket, provided by Abdulla, in his hand. Later that evening, railway workers came around to the first-class passenger guests to pass out bedding. Gandhi told the servant he did not need any bedding, as he had brought his own. Another first-class passenger noticed Gandhi and went to speak to railway officials about having an Indian riding in first class.

The officials came to speak to Gandhi and told him that he had to move to the van compartment, a section available to lesser-class ticket-holders. Gandhi had no intention of leaving the first-class compartment, since he had a first-class ticket. He told the officials he would not leave voluntarily and that they would have to physically remove him if they wanted him out of his compartment. The officials brought in a police officer, who took Gandhi by the hand and pushed him, along with his luggage, off the train.

Gandhi spent the night shivering from the cold winter night air in the waiting room of the Maritzburg railroad station, where he had been pushed off the train. (Maritzburg is the capital of Natal.) During his uncomfortable and humiliating stay, Gandhi thought about whether to remain in South Africa or to return to India. He decided he wanted to stay and fight against the discrimination he was experiencing. Yet the trip to Pretoria was far from over.

After being kicked off the train, Gandhi sent telegrams to the general manager of the railway station and also to Abdulla. Although the general manager defended the actions of the railway officials, he did see to it that Gandhi arrived to Charlestown via a second train without problems.

From Charlestown, Gandhi needed to take a stagecoach to Johannesburg, where he would then take a third train to his

RACISM IN NATAL

In the 1800s, racism in Africa was commonplace. White Europeans had established colonies throughout Africa, and they imposed their European beliefs and morals onto the Africans who lived there. The forty-three thousand Indians living in Natal in 1893 slightly outnumbered the forty thousand whites there. Both of these numbers were far less than the four hundred thousand native Zulus who lived in Natal. Nonetheless, the white Europeans held control over Natal and treated everyone else with contempt.

The English had established the colony of Natal in 1843. Indians began entering Natal in large numbers around 1850. These Indians had signed work contracts. These contracts held them responsible for working British-owned sugar or coffee plantations for a specified period of time for which they would be paid (usually a small sum). The Indians agreeing to these terms were the Untouchables. After the specified time, usually about five years, the Indians could decide to return to India or stay in Natal. Many of the indentured laborers chose to stay, becoming shopkeepers or farmers, and often flourishing in their businesses. In addition to the Untouchables, a number of higher-caste Indians also entered Natal to set up professional practices: businesses, law offices, and hospitals.

The Indians living in Natal began to outnumber the whites. Not only that, but the Indians were educated and were steadily growing wealthier. Their education and wealth posed a threat to the whites, who lashed out against the Indians and began to discriminate against them. Indians were not allowed to use the same bathrooms or drink water from the same fountains as whites. Indians were given lower-paying jobs and only had access to less-desirable housing. Gandhi spent his years in Africa trying to change these laws and bring equal rights to the Indians.

final destination of Pretoria. So, with ticket in hand, Gandhi approached the ticket agent for the stagecoach. The agent saw that Gandhi was Indian, and told him that his ticket had been canceled. The ticket agent then informed Gandhi that a coolie could not sit in the stagecoach with white passengers. If Gandhi wanted to ride the stagecoach, his only option was to ride on a seat outside, next to the driver. Because he did not want another confrontation, nor did he want to delay his trip any longer, Gandhi decided to take the outside seat.

But after beginning the journey, the white man in charge of the coach, who until this time had been riding inside the coach, decided he wanted to ride in Gandhi's spot so that he could enjoy the fresh air and smoke. The white man stopped the coach, placed a dirty cloth on the footboard, and told Gandhi to sit there so that the white man could sit in Gandhi's seat. Gandhi had had enough insult for one day and refused to sit at the white man's feet. The man began beating Gandhi and tried to drag him off the coach, but Gandhi clung to the stagecoach without returning any blows. The stagecoach passengers felt sorry for Gandhi and pleaded with the man to stop and let Gandhi ride inside with them. At last, the man agreed to let Gandhi continue his ride on a second outside seat and Gandhi was able to travel on to Johannesburg. By the end of the ordeal, Gandhi felt lucky to have arrived in Johannesburg in one piece.

Once in Johannesburg, Gandhi tried to get a hotel for the night, but discovered that the hotels were for whites only. In the morning, he learned that first-class train tickets from Johannesburg to Pretoria were not issued to Indians. Gandhi spoke to a ticket agent who took pity on Gandhi and decided to sell him a first-class ticket anyway. Once on the train, an angry official told Gandhi to move to third class. It did not matter to him that Gandhi held a first-class ticket. Luckily, an English passenger came to Gandhi's aid and told the official that he should let Gandhi be and that he didn't mind in the least riding with Gandhi. Before leaving, the official muttered, "If you want to travel with a coolie, what do I care?"[9]

After this treacherous journey that had begun in Natal, Gandhi at last arrived at Pretoria.

A CHANGE IN PLANS

After reaching Pretoria, Gandhi went about his business for Dada Abdulla, and before long, his year of agreed-upon work in South Africa was coming to a close. Gandhi would soon be sailing out of Natal to return home to India, where he would reunite with his wife and family. Before his departure, Abdulla threw Gandhi a huge going-away party. At the party, Gandhi happened to come across a newspaper article that explained how the Natal legislature was working to pass a law called the Franchise Amendment Bill. This law would strip Indians of their right to vote in South Africa. Gandhi and the other Indians at the party had been unaware of the pending proposal. When Gandhi asked the others what they thought about it, they responded that it was useless to try to fight the whites.

Gandhi felt differently. He told Abdulla, "This Bill, if it passes into law, will make our lot extremely difficult. It is the first nail into our coffin. It strikes at the root of our self-respect." [10] The other party guests recognized the truth in Gandhi's words. They asked Gandhi if he would extend his trip for one month to help them fight against this bill.

Gandhi had witnessed countless acts of racism during his year in South Africa. He knew that the passing of the Franchise Amendment Bill would be devastating to Indians. Indians had to stand up and fight against it or they would be, in essence, endorsing the whites' having a legal, superior position over Indians.

Gandhi agreed to extend his stay and began working against the bill immediately. He set up a meeting for Indians to plan their actions of opposition against the Franchise Amendment Bill. He asked Haji Muhammad, a well-respected leader of the Natal Indian community, to act as president of the meeting. Natal-born Indians, many of whom were Christian Indian youths, local Indian merchants, Hindus, Muslims, and others all came together to attend the meeting. They all wanted a better way of life and equal treatment in South Africa. At the meeting, Gandhi told them that, because Indians had not shown any opposition to the bill as of yet, it was about to be passed. They would need to move quickly.

The first thing the opposition group did was to send a telegram to the speaker of the Assembly, asking him to stop further discussion of the bill. The speaker granted a break of two days. Volunteers spent the entire night collecting signatures for their petition opposing the bill to be presented to the legislative Assembly. The petition created a stir in the community after it was published in the newspaper and widely discussed. Despite the talk it created, however, the bill passed.

Still, Gandhi and the others were not ready to give up. Their efforts had brought a new sense of unity among the Indians and they felt ready to stand up and fight. They set to work putting together a new petition that stated the Indian demands for equal rights. They hoped to get even greater numbers of signatures for this second petition. They were able to get ten thousand signatures, and the petition was sent to newspapers and also to Great Britain's secretary of state for the colonies in London. Gandhi hoped the group's efforts would lead to a veto of the bill.

The leaders of the Indian community greatly appreciated Gandhi's efforts. They asked him if he would be willing to stay in Natal permanently. Gandhi did not want to stay unless he could support himself as a lawyer and set up a household for himself. Once settled, Gandhi intended to send for his family to join him. Local merchants, about twenty in all, agreed to give Gandhi retainers for one year of legal work. In this way, Gandhi set up house.

LIFE IN NATAL

Gandhi purchased a two-story, five-bedroom home on the beachfront in a place called Beach Grove Villa. He wanted to live comfortably and in style, so he could show the whites that Indians were refined, cultured, and clean. Gandhi dressed meticulously, kept a beautiful house, and worked hard at his law practice—all of which went against the stereotypical white attitude about how Indians lived and behaved.

The Franchise Amendment Bill had passed and was not vetoed, despite the ten thousand signatures opposing it. But following through on the wave of Indian support for a better way of life among the Indians, Gandhi went about setting up an official organization that could give a voice to Indian concerns. On May 22, 1894, the Natal Indian Congress, of which Gandhi was secretary, was organized.

Gandhi's life in South Africa was going well. His involvement with the Natal Indian Congress allowed him to improve his own public relations skills, while helping others improve theirs, too. He taught Congress members how to listen and speak in the most efficient and effective ways. Gandhi's confidence grew, making him both a better public figure and lawyer. He became a symbol for defending the rights of minorities and was respected around the world.

With things going so smoothly in Natal, Gandhi felt he was ready to bring his wife and children to Africa. Gandhi had now been in South Africa for three years—two years longer than first agreed upon. But Gandhi was not finished in Natal. He wanted to stay and continue to push for a better way of life for the Indians who lived there. Gandhi requested permission to return to India for six months, during which he would gather his family and return with them to South Africa. Also during this time, he hoped to raise public awareness in India about what the living conditions were like for Indians in South Africa. Permission was granted and Gandhi set sail on the *Pongola*, headed for Calcutta, India. From Calcutta, he would board a train to take him to Bombay.

RETURN TO INDIA

In India once again, Gandhi did not waste any time getting the word out about what was happening in South Africa. Even before reaching his family, he stopped off in Rajkot and took a month to write *The Green Pamphlet*. This tract described, in detail, the condition of Indians in South Africa. Gandhi had ten thousand copies of the pamphlet printed. He sent them to every

Indian newspaper and political leader. When newspapers back in Natal printed their version of Gandhi's beliefs from *The Green Pamphlet*, they summarized Gandhi's words from the pamphlet, but with an exaggerated tone that caused many whites to take great offense to Gandhi's words.

When Gandhi was reunited at last with his family, he began preparing them for their trip to Natal. Gandhi felt his family had to look and act properly, according to the South African whites' standards, so that Gandhi would be taken seriously when he insisted on equal treatment for Indians. Gandhi instructed his wife to wear a Parsi sari, a dress made of a long piece of material that is draped around a woman's body to make a long skirt and a covering for the upper body, and his children to wear coats and pants. All of them had to begin wearing socks and shoes, which hurt their feet and to which they never fully became accustomed.

At last, Gandhi and his family set sail for Durban. After stormy weather aboard their ship, they pulled into port in January 1897. They were detained on board for medical examinations for five days. During this time, angry whites were gathering in Durban, still upset by what they believed Gandhi had said in *The Green Pamphlet*.

When Gandhi and his family stepped onto dry land, they were not greeted with open arms. A crowd began to swarm around Gandhi, separating him from the rest of his family. As Gandhi described it: "Then they pelted me with stones, brickbats and rotten eggs. Someone snatched away my turban, whilst others began to batter and kick me. I fainted and caught hold of the front railings of a house and stood there to get my breath. But it was impossible. They came upon me boxing and battering."[11] Someone managed to inform the police, who were able to take Gandhi and his family to safety.

Gandhi was strongly urged to press charges, but he refused. He said, "I do not want to prosecute anyone. . . . I do not hold the assailants to blame. They were given to understand that I had made exaggerated statements in India about the whites in Natal and calumniated them. If they believed these reports, it is no wonder that they were enraged."[12] Gandhi's words resulted in an outpouring of newfound respect and admiration for him. Just as he had done during the stagecoach incident on his way to Pretoria, Gandhi once again used passive resistance in response to a violent act.

Natal newspapers interviewed Gandhi and printed copies of the speeches that Gandhi had given while in India. All of Natal discovered that, indeed, Gandhi's speeches had been no stronger while he was in India than they had been during his first three years in South Africa. The whites felt ashamed of their actions and Gandhi was able to begin his second stay in Natal with greater support and backing.

As a result of what happened the day of Gandhi's return to Durban, Secretary of State for the Colonies Joseph Chamberlain pushed for the Natal legislature to pass a law that would give equal voting rights to all British subjects, which included Indians. The law was passed in 1897. It was a huge success for Gandhi.

5

Satyagraha

*The fight of Satyagraha is for the strong in spirit,
not the doubter or the timid. Satyagraha teaches us
the art of living as well as dying.*

—Mohandas Gandhi

Gandhi settled into life in South Africa with his family—Kasturbai (who was pregnant once again), nine-year-old Harilal, and five-year-old Manilal. One challenge he and Kasturbai had to face soon after their arrival was how to educate their children. One option was to send them to a Christian mission school. Normally reserved for European children, Indian children were not usually allowed to attend such schools. With Gandhi's influence, he could have been given an exception, but Gandhi did not want his children to learn strictly in English, nor did he want them to learn the ideals that the Christian missionary schools taught. Therefore, Gandhi made the decision to homeschool his children himself.

Gandhi was a practicing lawyer, a leader in the community, and a speaker in public affairs. All of this meant he had very little extra time to dedicate to the education of his children at home. Gandhi was often away, which caused large gaps in the continuity of his children's education. Finally, he decided that he had to hire a teacher, which he did, with the explicit requirement that the teacher work under Gandhi's supervision. Gandhi was still not satisfied. He went back to handling the children's instruction, however infrequent, himself.

Gandhi and Kasturbai had two more sons, both born in South Africa—Ramdas was born in 1897 and Devadas was born in 1900. Gandhi assisted with Ramdas's birth and actually delivered Devadas on his own. Gandhi educated all four boys himself. For a few months, Gandhi sent Harilal back to India for schooling, but then changed his mind and had his son return to South Africa. The boys eventually came to resent their father for keeping them from a public education, but Gandhi stood by his decision. He felt that although the education he gave his children was inadequate compared to public schools, the effects of a public education and the influence of Western ways would have been far worse for them. Gandhi wanted to instill in his children the same Hindu beliefs and morals that he held.

CHANGING VALUES

Until this time, Gandhi had believed that he had to act the part of a "civilized" European in order to give merit to being treated on equal terms with Europeans. His view changed, however. As had been the case in London, Gandhi continued to want to pare down his possessions and live more simply. He also wanted to cut down on his expenses. When he realized how much money he was spending on a washperson, he decided to launder his own clothes. He purchased a book on how to wash clothes and taught himself and Kasturbai how to clean and iron them. The same went for the barber—Gandhi began to cut his own hair after purchasing a pair of clippers. When he arrived at court after having cut his own hair for the first time, his friends asked him if rats had attacked his head.

Gandhi was taking on personal responsibilities that were not usually performed by individuals at his caste level. Only members of lower castes washed their own clothes and cut their own hair. In addition, Gandhi decided that his family should share the job of cleaning chamber pots. When he insisted that Kasturbai take a turn, she wanted no part in it, and they had a heated argument. Under Indian tradition, only Untouchables cleaned chamber pots, but Gandhi felt that custom should change. Gandhi did at last persuade his wife to clean the pot. All of the changes that Gandhi underwent during this time in his life stayed with him until his death.

During this time, war was brewing in South Africa. The British had been forcing their way onto Boer land and mining gold and diamonds. The Boers were descendants of Dutch settlers and had been farming the land in South Africa for hundreds of years. In 1899, war erupted between the British and Boer settlers. Gandhi felt that because he was fighting to gain rights equal to those of British citizens, he should help defend the British Empire. Personally, however, he sided with the Boers. And although Gandhi felt that all war was immoral, he nonetheless felt that his support of the British would help bring about improved conditions for the Indians.

Gandhi organized an Indian ambulance corps of eleven hundred members. The corps worked for six weeks, mostly outside the line of fire, attending the wounded. During the Battle at Spion Kop, the corps had to take greater risks when the battle grew fierce and there were many wounded. The corps did cross the firing line in order to carry wounded soldiers off the field and give them the medical attention they needed. Gandhi later won a medal for his service during the battle.

The war was not yet over—it would take three years until the Boers finally surrendered in 1902—but the British were thankful for the Indians' war efforts and relations between the two groups appeared to improve. Gandhi decided that his work in South Africa was coming to an end and he planned to return to India. He saw to it that his friends and colleagues would carry on his efforts to improve Indian conditions, and he promised to return to South Africa if his services were again needed. Gandhi then turned his attentions to his homeland of India.

BACK IN INDIA

When Gandhi prepared for his return to India, many of his friends from Natal brought him and his family lavish gifts of expensive jewelry, gold, and silver. Gandhi thought about his wife and children. "They were being trained to a life of service and to an understanding that service was its own reward."[13] Gandhi decided that the gifts should stay in Natal and be used to improve the well-being of the community. His children agreed with his reasoning, but Kasturbai was unhappy about returning the jewels. Over the years, she came to recognize his point of not needing such ornaments, but at the time, she was not pleased when Gandhi took it upon himself to deposit the jewels in a bank.

The Gandhis returned to their lives in India. Mohandas did quite a bit of traveling and, wherever he went, he spoke about the issues Indians faced in South Africa. During his travels, he met Gopal Krishna Gokhale, a well-liked Indian politician. Both Indians and British officials respected Gokhale. Gokhale later became Gandhi's close friend and mentor.

As Gandhi traveled across India, he became more and more aware of the similarities between his fight in South Africa for equal treatment between Indians and whites and the struggle in India between the castes and the Untouchables. While in Calcutta, Gandhi discovered that the delegates' lavatories were filthy. None of the delegates was willing to clean them and the Untouchables, who were the only people "able" to clean them, could not keep up with the constant cleaning required to maintain the overused lavatories, because they had other work to do as well. When Gandhi asked for a broom, the delegates were horrified. Still, he went about cleaning up a lavatory, since he had no intention of using it in the filthy condition in which he had found it.

Another time, while traveling by train from Calcutta to Rajkot, Gandhi purchased a third-class ticket so that he would get to see the difference between how third-class and first-class passengers were treated. The third-class passengers, mostly Untouchables, were bunched together in overcrowded cars; there was garbage on the floors; people smoked wherever they wanted, creating an unhealthful atmosphere; and there was a great deal of yelling and profanity.

Upon returning home once again, Gandhi found that his son Manilal, now ten years old, was very sick. He had typhoid and pneumonia and was quickly growing weaker, as his temperature rapidly increased. The doctor who had been called in recommended that the Gandhis give Manilal eggs and chicken broth to cure him. Gandhi informed the doctor that there was no way he was giving his son animal products. He wanted to know what his other options were. The doctor replied that he didn't believe there were any other options. Gandhi dismissed the doctor and took Manilal under his own care. He fed Manilal diluted orange juice for three days and gave him lots of short baths. When the boy's temperature didn't fall, Gandhi gave him a wet sheet pack. Gandhi later wrote, "I got up, wetted a sheet, wrung the water out of it and wrapped it about Manilal, keeping only his head out and then covered him with two blankets. To the head I applied a wet towel. The whole body was burning like hot iron, and quite parched. There was absolutely no perspiration." [14]

Gandhi left Manilal in his room and went out for a walk. He prayed while he was gone. When he returned, he found that Manilal's fever had broken and the child was perspiring once again. Manilal made a full recovery and grew up to be Gandhi's healthiest son.

RETURN TO SOUTH AFRICA

In November 1902, Gandhi was called back to South Africa. Joseph Chamberlain, British secretary of state for the colonies, was going to be visiting South Africa, and the Indians of Natal wanted Gandhi to meet with him to discuss the unfair treatment of Indians. Since the Boer War, relations between the whites and Indians had gone from bad to worse, and racial prejudice was soaring.

Gandhi agreed and presented Chamberlain with a list of complaints put together by Indians from various regions of South Africa. Gandhi did not receive the support he hoped for from Chamberlain and he realized that the battle for Indian equality was going to take a good deal more time and effort.

Gandhi traveled to Johannesburg, where times were especially hard for Indians. He decided that Johannesburg was where he was most needed and planned to set up a household. Kasturbai and their three youngest children joined him and Gandhi opened a new law office. Harilal had decided to remain in India and attend high school there, despite his father's opposition.

When not practicing law, Gandhi was with the poorest people in India. He treated the sick and lent a hand when needed. The pneumonic plague broke out in 1904. Fear of disease did not make Gandhi stop his visits among the poor, where the plague hit the strongest. Instead, he set up a makeshift hospital and nursed countless Indians back to health.

That same year, Gandhi began to publish a weekly newspaper called *Indian Opinion*, which was distributed throughout South Africa. Gandhi's main responsibility was overseeing the editorial columns, many of which he wrote himself. The articles were intended to inform the public about the Indian political cause and to bring attention to the health issues affecting poor Indians. Gandhi wanted to see the poor educated about hygienic living habits so that they could improve their overall health and standard of living. The articles in *Indian Opinion* also set straight any false rumors, which seemed to circulate regularly, about South African policies in regard to Indians.

TRUTH FORCE

Later in 1904, Gandhi set up a one-hundred-acre farm in Natal called the Phoenix Settlement. The main purpose of the farm was to save the *Indian Opinion*, which was in financial trouble. Gandhi reasoned that if he could gather a number of workers, including his family, they could live and work together to make the newspaper a success. Everyone living on the farm would be considered equal: Everyone would get the same amount of pay, share the farm chores, and work for the betterment of the community. In this way, Gandhi moved his family to the outskirts of Natal. Many of Gandhi's relatives also lived on the farm.

In 1906, the Zulu people of Natal were organizing a rebellion against the British. The Zulus had originally migrated to South Africa in the 1400s and were a Bantu-speaking people. The British were treating the Zulus unfairly and discriminating against them.

Once again, Gandhi organized his Indian ambulance corps, this time a smaller group of only twenty-four. As in the Boer War, Gandhi did not side with the British in his heart, but felt obligated to do so to further the Indian cause. Luckily for Gandhi, it turned out that he was able, under British orders, to aid the Zulus. White soldiers refused to help the wounded Zulus, so they passed the task on to the Indians. Gandhi later wrote, ". . . I was delighted, on reaching headquarters, to hear that our main work was to be the nursing of the wounded Zulus. The Medical Officer in charge welcomed us. He said the white people were not willing nurses for the wounded Zulus, that their wounds were festering, and that he was at his wit's end. . . . The Zulus were delighted to see us."[15]

Gandhi viewed the Zulu Rebellion as a manhunt, rather than a war. The British had mercilessly wounded and killed large numbers of Zulus. Gandhi was greatly disturbed by what he saw and it left a big impression on him. He felt he needed a life change. It was during the rebellion, which lasted only a few weeks, that Gandhi decided to take an ancient Hindu vow of self-control. The vow, called *brahmacharya*, included strict limits on what a person ate. From then on, Gandhi lived primarily on a diet of fresh fruit and nuts, as the food eaten under this vow should be raw and without spice. Gandhi wrote, "Eating is necessary only for sustaining the body and keeping it a fit instrument for service, and must never be practiced for self-indulgence. Food must therefore be taken, like medicine, under proper restraint. In pursuance of this principle one must eschew exciting foods, such as spices and condiments."[16]

Also as part of the vow, Gandhi and Kasturbai stopped all sexual relations. Gandhi explained: "If married, one must not have a carnal mind regarding one's wife or husband, but must consider her or him as one's lifelong friend, and establish relationship of perfect purity. A sinful touch, gesture or word is a direct breach of this principle."[17] The brahmacharya vow controlled outward energies and desires, such as food and sex, in order to build spiritual strength and make a person stronger.

Soon after taking his vow, Gandhi ran a contest in the *Indian Opinion* for the reader who could come up with a name for Gandhi's philosophy on the Indian movement toward equal treatment. Gandhi's cousin Magnanlal Gandhi won the contest with the name *sadagraha*, a Hindi word meaning "firmness in a good cause." Gandhi thought this word came very close to capturing the essence of the movement, but thought *satyagraha*, meaning "truth force" or "love force," was even clearer. *Satya* translates from Sanskrit to mean "truth and love" and *agraha* means "firmness" or "force." *Satyagraha* can also be defined as civil disobedience, passive resistance, or nonviolent noncooperation.

Satyagraha became the name of Gandhi's philosophy. This system of belief had been forming in Gandhi's mind over many years. It incorporated passive resistance, forgiveness, and tolerance. And above all else, satyagraha was about *ahimsa*, or "nonviolence." Gandhi felt that ahimsa meant much more than "nonviolence," however. He later wrote, "It really means that you may not offend anybody; you may not harbor an uncharitable thought, even in connection with one who may consider himself to be your enemy."[18] Gandhi considered ahimsa a complete way of life—one he would live by for the rest of his life.

ASIATIC REGISTRATION BILL

New laws were being proposed in South Africa. The Asiatic Registration Bill, which Indians referred to as the "Black Act," would require Indian and Chinese people over the age of eight to register with South African officials and get fingerprinted. They would be forced to carry a permit; if they were found without the proper permit, they could be fined, imprisoned, or deported from South Africa. Gandhi was appalled by the proposed law, and left immediately for London, where he hoped to convince British officials to stop the bill from being passed.

Back in South Africa, Gandhi attended a meeting in Johannesburg in September 1906. Gandhi spoke to three thousand Indians at the Empire Theatre. He encouraged all Indians to join a mass resistance movement against the Black Act. Yet he did not want the people to make the decision not to register lightly. "If . . . we violate our pledge we are guilty before God and man. . . . If you have not the will or the ability to stand firm even when you are perfectly isolated you must not . . . take the pledge."[19] Despite his warning, everyone in attendance at the meeting pledged not to register. Not quite a year later, on July 1, 1907, the South African government passed the Asiatic Registration Bill into law.

About six months after the Black Act had been passed, the government began to arrest those people who were not carrying their passes. Gandhi did not carry a permit, because he had pledged not to. He was arrested and put in jail during the week of Christmas, 1907. He used the time behind bars to read.

The South African jails were filling up. The government realized that it would not be able to jail all of the protesters who refused to carry a permit. The British government then told Indians that the Black Act would be withdrawn if the Indians would register voluntarily. Gandhi was one of the first to do so and others followed his example. After the Indians had registered, however, the government said it would not withdraw the Black Act. Gandhi immediately organized a public bonfire in which three thousand protesters gathered to burn their permits. The police arrived and began to beat up the protesters, including Gandhi, and the Indians were returned to prison. When Gandhi completed his second jail sentence, he once again took to protesting the permit law and was once again thrown in jail.

For years, Gandhi worked to put an end to the Black Act, but to no avail. Then, in 1910, he organized a new settlement outside Johannesburg, similar to the Phoenix Settlement in Natal. He called it Tolstoy Farm, after one of Gandhi's influences, Russian novelist Leo Tolstoy. Like Gandhi, Tolstoy believed in nonviolence as a method of creating change. In writing about why Tolstoy Farm was established, one biographer wrote: "Tolstoy Farm was both a gesture of idealism and a response to political necessity, as by this time the families of those who had followed Gandhi into passive resistance and jail needed homes and maintenance."[20]

In 1912, Gandhi's friend G. K. Gokhale arrived in South Africa from India. He had come to observe the Indians' living conditions. During Gokhale's visit, Gandhi spent a great deal of time with him. Gandhi wanted to be certain that Gokhale witnessed the hardships that Indians were facing in South Africa. Gandhi also brought Gokhale to Tolstoy Farm and showed him the ashram's accomplishments. After Gokhale toured South Africa, he was able to convince the government to promise to drop an Indian tax and repeal the Asiatic Registration Bill. Neither promise was kept. Later that year, Tolstoy Farm closed and its farmers went to live on the Phoenix Settlement in Natal.

In 1913, a new law announced that only Christian marriages had legal status in South Africa, which made Indian marriages null and void. Indians were justifiably outraged. Gandhi and his followers began a series of marches across South Africa to demonstrate the injustice of the laws against Indians.

LIFE AT TOLSTOY FARM AND THE INFLUENCES BEHIND IT

Mohandas Gandhi greatly admired the Russian writer Leo Tolstoy. When Gandhi first arrived in South Africa, he read one of Tolstoy's books, *The Kingdom of God Is Within You*. This book made a lasting impression on Gandhi. It talked about finding truth and love within one's heart. For Gandhi, the book reinforced his ideal of nonviolence as a way of life. Gandhi was so impressed by Tolstoy's book that he wrote a series of letters to Tolstoy, beginning in 1909. Tolstoy responded to Gandhi's final letter from his deathbed. Gandhi received it a few days after Tolstoy's death in 1910.

Gandhi and his family lived and worked at Tolstoy Farm, where he was able to put Tolstoy's ideas into practice in everyday life. The Gandhis owned hardly any possessions; they were completely self-reliant; they ate meals consisting primarily of bananas, lemons, dates, and raw ground nuts; they made their own clothing, including sandals; they treated everyone as equals; they accepted no gifts of value; and they used only herbal remedies and natural methods of healing.

Gandhi treated education with the utmost respect. He and the other adults on the farm taught the children of the ashram. The children's education included hands-on farm work during the day, academic work taught in the evenings, and religious studies taught throughout the day. Gandhi felt that children gained the best part of their education outside the classroom. He believed parents were the best qualified to teach their own personal beliefs and morals to their children, but he also felt that children should be taught tolerance of others' beliefs and morals. The days on Tolstoy Farm were grueling and long, but they were spiritually satisfying and mentally fulfilling. All the residents on the farm worked together and were there for one another.

Finally, on June 26, 1914, the Indian Relief Bill was passed. With this bill, Indian and Muslim marriages were recognized and some unfair taxes that had been placed on Indians were removed.

With this success, Gandhi felt that his work in South Africa was complete. It was time to go home. On July 18, 1914, Mohandas and Kasturbai Gandhi set sail on an eighteen-day journey for England, which they planned to visit before returning to India. They would never again go back to South Africa.

6

Returning to India

*My patriotism is not an exclusive thing. It is
all-embracing, and I should reject that patriotism
which sought to mount the distress or
exploitation of other nationalities.*

—Mohandas Gandhi

World War I began in the summer of 1914. Many causes contributed to the outbreak of the war—primarily imperialistic, territorial, and economic rivalries, as well as growing nationalism. Great Britain entered the war at the beginning of August, just two days before Gandhi and Kasturbai arrived in England. The trip from South Africa to England had gone well. Gandhi now made it a point always to travel third-class, even though this usually meant he endured dirty, overcrowded conditions. He continued to want to know how the lowest classes were treated and felt he should experience what they experienced. The third-class trip on this ship, however, was clean and the steward supplied the Gandhis with fruit and nuts, which usually was not done.

Upon his arrival in England, Gandhi set to work putting together his third Indian ambulance corps. Volunteers to the corps, numbering about eighty, spent six weeks learning first aid in preparation for their service. Gandhi also helped the war effort by sewing clothes for the soldiers.

Some of Gandhi's friends questioned his involvement in the war. They considered it going against his ideas of peace. But Gandhi felt he had three options:

> I could declare open resistance to the war and, in accordance with the law of Satyagraha, boycott the Empire until it changed its military policy; or I could seek imprisonment by civil disobedience of such of its laws as were fit to be disobeyed; or I could participate in the war on the side of the Empire and thereby acquire the capacity and fitness for resisting the violence of war. I lacked this capacity and fitness, so I thought there was nothing for it but to serve in the war. [21]

Just as he had felt during the Boer War, Gandhi believed that if Indians showed support for the British, Great Britain would show its appreciation by improving conditions for the Indians.

Gandhi's involvement in the war, however, was cut short by an illness called pleurisy, a painful respiratory disease caused by breathing damp, cold air. Gandhi, Kasturbai, and their children were advised to return to the warmer climate of India. By the time they reached Bombay on January 9, 1915, Gandhi was already feeling much better. He and his family were met by a large reception of well-wishers. It had been twelve years since Gandhi had first said good-bye to his family when he left for South Africa. Now he was home to stay.

MAHATMA

In 1915, people began to call Gandhi *Mahatma*, meaning "Great Soul." Gandhi's only desire was to help his people. Although he was a wealthy lawyer, Mahatma Gandhi lived as a poor peasant. He gave his earnings to Phoenix Settlement or Tolstoy Farm or put it into the community. He owned almost no possessions. He ate what he grew from the earth. He gave speeches about the equality of all people, urging Indians to put an end to the caste system. He wanted a peaceful India in which people respected one another and valued each other's differences. Mahatma Gandhi dedicated his life to the service of India's people.

After arriving in India, Gandhi first traveled to the city of Poona, near Bombay, where his longtime friend, Gokhale, was staying. Gokhale was in poor health and thought to be near death. Gokhale told Gandhi to take a year to travel around India and get to know its people again before getting into politics. Gandhi agreed. After his visit with Gokhale, Gandhi and Kasturbai visited relatives in Rajkot and Porbandar. Then he began his travels to become more acquainted with India's people. Not long after he began, he received news of Gokhale's death. Gandhi returned for the funeral and to spend some time mourning for his close friend. Gokhale's death was a great loss for Gandhi.

After Gandhi's return to Poona, he resumed his travels around India. Of the 300 million people living in India at the time, only a small fraction was without hardship; the majority of India's people lived in poverty—often, in extreme poverty. Huge slums could be found in all of India's major cities. Homeless people were a common sight. Gandhi was saddened by what he saw on his travels. He was constantly subjected to sanitation problems, disease, joblessness and homelessness, and an overwhelming feeling of despair. It was an eye-opening period in Gandhi's life, and one that he would never forget.

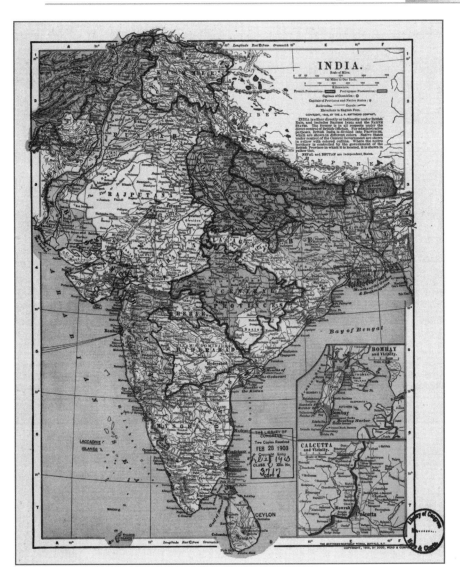

This 1903 map of India shows the subcontinent as it was divided under British rule.

SATYAGRAHA ASHRAM

In addition to learning about the people, Gandhi was also using this time of travel to find a place to establish a new ashram like the Phoenix Settlement and the Tolstoy Farm. Gandhi defined an *ashram* as "a community of men of religion."[22] It was a place where people lived together as one family. Already about twenty people who had been living at Gandhi's Phoenix Settlement in South Africa had come to India, wanting to resettle there. Until now, they had been staying at Santiniketan, a school founded by Rabindranath Tagore, an Indian poet.

Gandhi decided to locate the new ashram along the Sabarmati River at Kochrab. The site was near the city of Ahmedabad, which was the oldest manufacturing city in India. He liked it because "... as Ahmedabad was an ancient centre of handloom weaving, it was likely to be the most favourable field for the revival of the cottage industry of hand-spinning. There was also the hope that, the city being the capital of Gujarat, monetary help from its wealthy citizens would be more available here than elsewhere."[23] On May 25, 1915, the Satyagraha Ashram was founded. Each member of the new ashram took a vow of truth, nonviolence, chastity, and control of the palate.

Soon after Satyagraha Ashram started, Gandhi was faced with an unexpected request. An Untouchable family, consisting of Dudabhai, Danibehn, and their daughter, Lakshmi, wished to join the new ashram. At the time, there were about thirteen families living there, including Gandhi, his wife, and their children. Gandhi approached the others at Satyagraha Ashram and asked what they thought about the request. They thought the ashram should accept the family. Gandhi later wrote, "I wrote to Amritlal Thakkar expressing our willingness to accept the family, provided all the members were ready to abide by the rules of the Ashram."[24]

Gandhi's acceptance of an Untouchable family into Satyagraha Ashram caused concern among the supporters of the ashram. The monetary support that the ashram had received up to this point stopped. The ashram was at risk of having to shut down. To save money and boycott against the supporters' discrimination toward Dudabhai and his family, Gandhi told the other members of the ashram that they would all live together in Dudabhai's quarters. Gandhi hoped to show the former monetary supporters that he and his followers would not be pushed out of their ashram. But some members of the ashram did not like being told that they were going to live closely with Dudabhai and his family. It was one thing to share the ashram with Untouchables, but for some, it was quite another to live in the same house. Indians had grown up believing in and having trust in the caste system. Some threatened to leave.

Gandhi worried that he would be forced to move Satyagraha Ashram. Then, the ashram received an anonymous donation that would allow it to function for another year. Dudabhai and his family remained at the ashram and relations between the family and the rest of the members improved as everyone learned about tolerance and acceptance. In the years following, numerous Untouchable families joined and were warmly welcomed at Satyagraha Ashram.

SATYAGRAHA CAMPAIGNS IN INDIA

Since Gandhi's arrival back in India, he had been silent in politics; he had concentrated instead on getting to know the people of India and taking note of what changes he thought were needed. He visited farmers in India's countryside; he visited peasants in the mountains; and he visited beggars and laborers in the city's slums. Gandhi listened to the people talk about their hardships and thought of ways to improve their conditions. Mainly, he wanted to see improved sanitation conditions, a healthier life-style, and better education. Wherever he went, Gandhi worked alongside those he spoke to, cleaning latrines, working in textile mills, or sewing clothes.

In 1917, Gandhi traveled to Champaran, a rural district in Bihar near the Himalaya Mountains. The peasants who lived in Champaran worked for British indigo planters. The British, who owned the land that the peasants farmed, allotted 15 percent of the land for growing indigo and then took the entire indigo crop as payment for rent of the land. When Gandhi and some of his companions arrived at Champaran, the peasants welcomed them into their homes. Gandhi later wrote of the peasants at Champaran, "No political work had yet been done amongst them. The world outside Champaran was not known to them.

And yet they received me as though we had been age-long friends. It is no exaggeration, but the literal truth, to say that in this meeting with the peasants I was face to face with God, Ahimsa [nonviolence] and Truth." [25]

After Gandhi arrived in Champaran and began to listen to the peasants' complaints, the police department took notice of Gandhi's actions. The police superintendent informed Gandhi that he had to leave the area immediately. Gandhi politely declined. The police superintendent then told Gandhi that he would have to report to court the following day. Crowds of people showed up at the courthouse. They wanted to see the Mahatma set free. Not wanting to cause a greater stir among the peasants, the magistrate sent word to Gandhi that the lieutenant governor had withdrawn the case. Gandhi was again free to continue his study of the indigo growers.

Gandhi's work at Champaran became his first use of satyagraha, or "truth force," in India. Gandhi and his volunteers spent much of their time educating the peasants about ways they could fight peacefully for their rights; organizing schools for the children; and preaching the benefits of good sanitation. The hard work of Gandhi's first satyagraha campaign in India brought success. After listening to Gandhi's speeches and reading his letters about the conditions at Champaran, the government agreed to a partial monetary reimbursement for the peasant farmers.

A year had passed since Gandhi had left Satyagraha Ashram, though he returned for short visits now and then. But when he learned of a pressing problem in the city of Ahmedabad, located near the Satyagraha Ashram, he left Champaran. Unfortunately, his departure from Champaran put a stop to many of the projects he had helped the peasants begin. Schools and hospitals began to shut down without Gandhi's guidance. It saddened Gandhi to see much of his work undone, but he had no choice but to turn his attentions to Ahmedabad.

Arriving in Ahmedabad at the beginning of 1918, Gandhi learned that there was trouble between the textile workers and the mill owners. The thousands of workers received little pay and lived in near-slum conditions. The mill owners were not willing to increase the workers' pay, however. Gandhi believed in the following five conditions of labor:

> 1. The hours of labor must leave the workmen some hours of leisure; 2. They must get facilities for their own education; 3. Provision should be made for an adequate supply of milk, clothing and necessary education for their children; 4. There should be sanitary dwellings for the workmen; 5. They should be in a position to save enough to maintain themselves during their old age. [26]

But he found that none of these five conditions was being met. Gandhi recommended to the workers that they go on strike.

Around this same time, a plague broke out in the nearby city of Kochrab, where the Satyagraha Ashram was located. Gandhi wrote, "It was impossible to keep ourselves immune from the effects of the surrounding insanitation, however scrupulously we might observe the rules of cleanliness within the Ashram walls." [27]

Gandhi decided it was necessary to move Satyagraha Ashram to a new location. He heard about a site located near the Sabarmati Central Jail. Gandhi thought this would be an ideal location, as ". . . jails have generally clean surroundings." [28] The land was bought and the forty people living at Satyagraha Ashram began moving to their new location.

Gandhi was still overseeing the textile workers' strike in Ahmedabad at this time. The strike continued for two weeks. The workers had pledged not to go back to work unless their terms were accepted or the mill owners agreed to arbitration. But no agreement was made and the workers began to get anxious. Gandhi worried they would go back on their pledge and return to work at the same low rates. Gandhi told them to pull together and continue the strike until an agreement was reached. If they didn't, he would refuse to eat. The workers were stunned and apologized to Gandhi for wavering, promising not to break their pledge. The workers told Gandhi he should not fast, but they should. Gandhi told them to be strong. He said it was necessary for them to fast as long as they stood by the strike, but that Gandhi would not eat until the strike was settled.

As Satyagraha Ashram was in the middle of moving to its new location, much work was being done. Gandhi's cousin Magnanlal suggested giving some of the striking textile workers jobs; the workers could help carry sand from the river to the building site for the ashram's new weaving school. The sand would be used to lay the foundation of the school. Gandhi later wrote that one of the female textile workers " . . . led the way with a basket on her head and soon an endless stream of labourers carrying baskets of sand on their heads could be seen issuing out of the hollow of the river-bed. It was a sight worth seeing. The labourers felt themselves infused with a new strength, and it became difficult to cope with the task of paying out wages to them." [29]

Gandhi's fast had to last only three days. After twenty-one days of striking, a settlement was reached between the textile workers and the mill owners. The mill owners agreed to a slight wage increase for the workers. This had been Mahatma Gandhi's first use of a public fast as a means of satyagraha.

END OF WORLD WAR I

At this time, Gandhi still held the belief that if Indians showed their loyalty to the British government by staying involved in World War I, the British would respond by granting the Indians independence. In 1918, Gandhi continued to try to recruit Indians to fight in the war.

During his recruiting efforts, Gandhi became very ill with a disease called dysentery, severe diarrhea mixed with blood. His body became so weak, he was unable to get out of bed. Doctors were called and most suggested various diets that included meat broth or eggs. Gandhi refused. Another doctor recommended covering his body with ice packs, which Gandhi tried. But the dysentery continued and Gandhi's already weak body was failing. Finally, after agreeing to drink goat's milk, Gandhi's body slowly began to heal after months of serious illness. Gandhi gradually regained his strength.

World War I ended in November 1918, while Gandhi was still sick. He remained weak months later, in fact, in 1919, when he learned about the passing of the Rowlatt Bill. This bill would give the British government the right to investigate any person or persons who acted against or said anything against the British government. Indians across the country were outraged. Gandhi was upset that the British did not plan to repay the Indians for their service in the war with independence. He could see that Great Britain intended to keep its rule over India. Gandhi felt a new strength to get well—he felt he must get healthy and protest against the injustice of the Rowlatt Bill.

KHEDA CAMPAIGN

In March 1918, just after the Ahmedabad textile workers' strike was over, Gandhi was called to another satyagraha campaign. This one was for the peasants living in the district of Kheda, located in the western region of Gujarat. The peasants had been faced with crop failures that resulted in near-famine conditions. As a result, the peasants were asking the British government to cancel the taxes on the crops, because the peasants could not afford to pay the taxes. The government insisted that the crop figures were enough to merit the taxes and refused to cancel them.

Gandhi arrived in Kheda and spent his time listening to both the peasants and the landowners and observing the living conditions around him. Following his observations, Gandhi suggested to the peasants that they begin a satyagraha campaign. Gandhi's presence in Kheda was noticed by most of the people in Gujarat. They closely followed Gandhi's work on the campaign.

Gandhi and his volunteers then focused their energies on educating the Kheda peasants about satyagraha. They taught the peasants how to organize marches and peaceful demonstrations. They taught the peasants about the importance of healthy living. The Kheda campaign came to an end when the British government agreed to tax only the wealthiest of the peasants; the poorer peasants were exempt from paying the tax.

The real benefit of the Kheda campaign came from its teachings about satyagraha to the Gujarat region as a whole. Gandhi later wrote, "The Kheda Satyagraha marks the beginning of an awakening among the peasants of Gujarat, the beginning of their true political education. . . . Through the Kheda campaign Satyagraha took firm root in the soil of Gujarat."*

Source: Mohandas K. Gandhi, *An Autobiography: The Story of My Experiments with Truth*, Boston: Beacon Press, 1957, p. 440.

7

Moving Toward Swaraj

Many people exult at the explosion of bombs. This only shows ignorance. . . . If all the British were to be killed, those who kill them would become the masters of India, and . . . India would continue in a state of slavery.

—Radical Indian reform activist Bal Gangadhar Tilak

Despite months of the Indians' protesting of the Rowlatt Bill, the bill passed into law. In response, Gandhi suggested a nationwide satyagraha. In cities and towns across India, the satyagraha would start off with a *hartal*, or strike, during which Indians would close their businesses in order to fast and pray in protest of the Rowlatt Act. Gandhi later wrote, "The idea came to me last night in a dream that we should call upon the country to observe a general hartal. Satyagraha is a process of self-purification, and ours is a sacred fight, and it seems to me to be in the fitness of things that it should be commenced with an act of self-purification."[30]

Gandhi began a public tour in southern India to speak against the Rowlatt Act and to inform people about the nationwide satyagraha. He founded his second newspaper, this one called *Young India*, in which he wrote articles about the Rowlatt Act and what people could do to protest it.

Although it appeared that many people planned to join the satyagraha campaign and take part in the hartal, the strikes across India were not all peaceful. In numerous cities, including Delhi, Lahore, and Ahmedabad, violence erupted. Gandhi made speeches against the violence, telling the people that riots and lootings were not the way of satyagraha, but despite his pleas, the violence was out of control and could not be stopped.

In Amritsar, Indians attacked British schools and churches. Angry Indians assaulted a female British teacher and killed five British men. The fighting reached a climax on April 13, 1919. Close to six thousand Indians were gathered in the city of Amritsar to protest the Rowlatt Act; the streets were filled with people. Suddenly, British soldiers pulled out machine guns and opened fire on the large masses of unarmed Indians, killing 379 people and wounding more than one thousand others. Indians dubbed this incident the "Amritsar Massacre." Today, a plaque hangs at the location where the gunfire first erupted. It reads: "To the martyrdom of fifteen hundred Sikhs, Hindus and Moslems, killed and wounded by British bullets."[31]

Gandhi was deeply saddened by the violent event. He also changed his views about the British. He said, "I had faith in them—until 1919 . . . but the Amritsar Massacre . . . changed my heart."[32]

To demonstrate his dissatisfaction with the British government, Gandhi returned two medals he had received from the British for his participation in the Boer War and the Zulu Rebellion. He no longer wished to show his cooperation with Great Britain. He asked other Indians to follow his lead and return any war decorations they may have received from the British as well.

FIGHT AGAINST BRITISH RULE

Gandhi's new change of heart led him to seek *swaraj*, or "self-rule," through satyagraha. But after seeing the violence erupt across India in previous months, he knew that he would first need to educate many more of India's 300 million people about satyagraha principles. The Indian National Congress supported Gandhi's views and helped bring recognition to the cause. Gandhi also worked to include the Indian Muslims within the satyagraha campaign. Muslims and Hindus had a history of not standing together, but Gandhi hoped to see all people in India unite to bring about their independence. As part of this process, Gandhi wanted to abolish the idea of Untouchability.

Gandhi encouraged the boycotting of British goods. Indians, with Gandhi right alongside them, attended public demonstrations where they removed their British-made clothes and burned them in large bonfires. Gandhi also urged Indians to stop paying their taxes, to stop attending British-run schools and universities, and to stop working in public offices. People marched in the streets. Sometimes these demonstrations ended in violence and rioting, although Gandhi continually spoke against this and often went on fasts to show his disapproval.

The majority of India's people worshiped Gandhi. Many believed he was a saint. People all over the world compared Gandhi's life to that of Jesus Christ. When villagers and townspeople heard of Gandhi's arrival to their area, they made a point of trying to catch sight of him, touch him, or speak to him. When they got close enough, they bowed at his feet. Gandhi often joked about his being viewed as a saint or god-like figure. He was a modest, humble man who did not see himself in that way.

When Gandhi traveled across India to speak about his beliefs and educate Indians about satyagraha and other causes, masses of

KHADI

One way in which Gandhi hoped to obtain nonviolent noncooperation, or civil disobedience, against the British was to encourage people to boycott the purchase of British goods. In order to do this, he would need to convince people that they could get by without the British goods. Previously, Gandhi and the other members of his ashram had figured out a way to clothe themselves from cloth made entirely by hand. To do this, they learned to spin cotton on a *charkha*, or spinning wheel. This produced a yarn called *khadi*, which was much rougher, but much cheaper, than the finer cotton the British manufactured and then sold to Indians for a high price. Gandhi began wearing nothing but a *dhoti*, a kind of loincloth similar to shorts, made of khadi, along with a pair of handmade sandals. When it was cold, he would drape another piece of khadi cloth over his shoulder, much like a shawl.

Gandhi traveled around India to teach people how to spin khadi and make their own clothes. He saw khadi as a means of helping India out of its extreme poverty. About khadi he wrote,

> My work should be . . . to organize the production of hand-spun cloth, and to find means for the disposal of the Khadi thus produced. I am . . . concentrating my attention on the production of Khadi . . . because through it I can provide work to the semi-starved, semi-employed women of India. My idea is to get these women to spin yarn, and to clothe the people of India with Khadi woven out of it.*

Thus khadi became a symbol of Indian independence.

Source: Mohandas K. Gandhi, *An Autobiography: The Story of My Experiments with Truth*, Boston: Beacon Press, 1957, p. 496.

people gathered to listen to him speak. Gandhi was a small man with a soft-spoken voice. Some people, expecting a passionate, boisterous speech, were disappointed when they first heard him speak. Some criticized what he said, but others lived by it.

Despite Gandhi's popularity, violence continued. In February 1921, a riot broke out in the village of Chauri Chaura. Twenty-two police officers were killed after protesters set fire to the police station. Gandhi could not understand the violence. He fasted for five days and continued writing in *Young India* about his views opposing violence—but opposing the British government as well. He was appointed leader of the Indian National Congress that year, which gave him executive power. The National Congress informed Gandhi that he would select his own successor, when the time came.

On March 10, 1922, Gandhi was arrested for sedition, or inciting rebellion. The British government felt that the articles he had published in *Young India* criticized the British Empire, which violated the Rowlatt Act. He attended trial in Ahmedabad, where he pleaded guilty to all charges. At the close of the trial, Gandhi was sentenced to six years in Yeravda Prison, located in Poona. He entered the prison on March 18, 1922.

Gandhi spent his years in prison spinning, praying, and reading more than one hundred fifty books and plays. When he was diagnosed with appendicitis and needed an emergency operation, he was released from prison four years early. The government was worried that if Gandhi were to die in jail, the backlash from India's people would be too great for the government to handle. And so, at fifty-five years of age, Mahatma Gandhi was back in the public light.

FAMILY LIFE

During the two years Gandhi spent in prison, India changed. Tensions between Muslims and Hindus had risen. A riot broke out between the Muslims and Hindus in Kohat. Gandhi was so disturbed by the bitterness between the two groups that he began a twenty-one-day fast. He held his fast in Delhi at the home of his good friend Maulana Mahomed Ali, a Muslim. Biographer Judith Brown wrote,

> He ended the fast on the due day with his particular talent for theatre and symbolism. . . . All morning crowds of people flocked . . . to watch the climax, and Gandhi insisted that even the servants should be allowed to attend, making a point of giving special thanks to the sweeper. . . . Gandhi was so weak his words to his Muslim friends were barely audible; the ceremony ended with him drinking a glass of orange juice.[33]

It would be months before Gandhi fully recovered from his weight loss and regained his energy.

Gandhi felt that he needed some time away from the public. He returned to the Satyagraha Ashram and, during 1925, did not do any public speaking. Kasturbai, during these years in India, continued to stand faithfully by her husband. Gandhi and Kasturbai maintained a good relationship during their later years of marriage. Gandhi later wrote, "We have had numerous bickerings, but the end has always been peace between us. The wife, with her matchless powers of endurance, has always been the victor."[34]

The couple had concerns, however, especially with their oldest son, Harilal. Harilal seemed prone to bad influences. Biographer Martin Green wrote that Harilal "alternately denied and betrayed his father's moral teaching. For thirty or forty years Harilal increasingly played the rogue, quarreling bitterly with his father, semideliberately destroying himself by an addiction to drink and drugs and other vices, and once renounced Hinduism for Islam."[35]

Gandhi's second son, Manilal, had returned to South Africa, where he took charge of the Phoenix Settlement and edited *Indian Opinion*. When Manilal fell in love with a Muslim woman, Gandhi did not approve. He did not think marriages between Hindus and Muslims would help Hindu-Muslim social and political relations. Instead, Gandhi arranged a marriage for Manilal with a Hindu woman. Both Harilal and Manilal resented their father's upbringing of them and never had very close relationships with their father, although Manilal did agree with and help fight for many of the same causes that Gandhi did.

Gandhi's closest relationships were with his third son, Ramdas, and his youngest son, Devadas. Unfortunately, Ramdas was often in poor health and never found a job to settle into. Both Ramdas and Devadas supported their father's work and often attended marches and demonstrations at his side.

DECLARATION OF INDEPENDENCE

On November 8, 1927, the British assembled a committee called the Simon Commission, with its purpose being to review India's constitution and suggest changes. Its seven members were all British; it was headed by Sir John Simon. Not a single Indian was asked to sit in on the commission. When the commission arrived in India one year later, it was met with resistance from the Indians. People marched the streets carrying black flags that read "Simon Go Back."

Indian politicians got together to form an All Parties Conference. At Gandhi's suggestion, the group decided to write their own constitution for India. The constitution was called the Nehru Report, after Indian political leader Motilal Nehru. Jawaharlal Nehru, son of Motilal Nehru, would succeed Gandhi as leader of the Indian National Congress. The two Nehrus, with other political leaders, worked together to draft the report. The Nehru Report suggested that India become a dominion, meaning it would recognize the king of England as chief of state, but India would be a self-governing nation. The report also stated that if the report were not accepted by December 31, 1929, India would again move into a nonviolent noncooperation movement and seek complete swaraj.

Biographer Judith Brown noted, "Gandhi, with his professed lack of interest in constitutional schemes, whether emanating from British or Indian pens, took no part in the All Parties Conference and its work, though he was always present behind the scenes and was kept informed of developments by the two

Nehrus."[36] Gandhi did speak out on behalf of the Nehru Report, showing his support and educating Indians about its contents. Gandhi's main objective at this time, however, was to continue to encourage national unity, which he felt was necessary if India were to achieve swaraj.

Gandhi met with Lord Irwin, the viceroy of India, on December 23, 1929. At the meeting, Gandhi discovered that Great Britain did not plan to accept India as a dominion and was going to reject the Nehru Report. Gandhi immediately declared India's independence, and Jawaharlal Nehru unveiled a new flag that would represent a free India. On January 26, 1930, Indians celebrated Independence Day. The struggle for an independent India, however, would actually go on for another seventeen years.

THE SALT MARCH

The British government had imposed a law, called the Salt Act, in 1882 that allowed a British monopoly on the collection and manufacturing of salt in India. Gandhi decided to protest the law by bringing seventy-eight of his followers on a march from his Satyagraha Ashram to a small village called Dandi, located on the west coast of India. Once there, he would remove salt from the Arabian Sea, thus breaking the law. This march of satyagraha would be done in the name of swaraj.

Gandhi explained to the people why he was protesting the salt tax: "Next to air and water, salt is perhaps the greatest necessity of life. It is the only condiment of the poor. . . . There is no article like salt outside water by taxing which the State can reach even the starving millions, the sick, the maimed and the utterly helpless. The tax constitutes therefore the most inhuman poll tax that ingenuity of man can devise."[37] The salt tax upset Gandhi most because it affected the poorest people of India the hardest.

Gandhi wrote a letter to Lord Irwin, informing him of his intention to march from Ahmedabad to Dandi and then to break the law by taking salt from the sea. Gandhi believed in always being truthful and upfront. The purpose of the salt march was not to cause undue upheaval; therefore, he made sure to include his entire itinerary of the event, so that Lord Irwin would not be faced with any surprises. Lord Irwin did not reply, but his secretary sent the following message: "His Excellency . . . regrets to learn that you contemplate a course of action which is clearly bound to involve violation of the law and danger to the public peace."[38] Gandhi's reply to this message was, "On bended knee I asked for bread, and I received stone instead."[39]

In the days that followed Gandhi's famous 241-mile march and taking of salt from the sea, thousands of people arrived in Dandi and other coastal cities to make salt. Jawaharlal Nehru later wrote, "As we saw the abounding enthusiasm of the people and the way salt-making was spreading like a prairie fire, we felt a little abashed and ashamed for having questioned the efficacy of this method when it was first proposed by Gandhiji [Gandhi]."[40] And biographer Louis Fischer wrote, "Every villager on India's long seacoast went to the beach or waded into the sea with a pan to make salt. The police began mass arrests. Ramdas, third son of Gandhi, with a large group of ashramites, was arrested."[41] By the end of the protest, about sixty thousand Indians were arrested and jailed for their involvement in the removal of salt from Indian waters.

Just after midnight on May 4, Mahatma Gandhi, too, was arrested in Karadi, a village located near Dandi. He was sent, once again, to Yeravda Prison in Poona, where he resumed his spinning, praying, and reading.

8

Continued Unrest

The cry of "Quit India" . . . comes not from the lips
but from the aching hearts of millions.

—Mohandas Gandhi

G andhi had been given no trial before being sent to prison in 1930. During Gandhi's prison term, Indian poet Sarojini Naidu led twenty-five hundred volunteers in a demonstration at Dharasana Salt Works. Naidu would later become the only woman on the Congress Working Committee. She and Gandhi were close friends, and she worked as one of his chief aides.

About half a mile away from Dharasana, Naidu had these words for her volunteers: "Gandhi's body is in jail but his soul is with you. India's prestige is in your hands. You must not use any violence under any circumstances. You will be beaten but you must not resist; you must not even raise a hand to ward off blows."[42] Among the demonstrators was Gandhi's second son, Manilal.

The heat was unbearable that day, reaching 116°F. The demonstrators approached Dharasana Salt Works slowly and methodically. They showed no fear and no violence. Salt deposits, protected by surrounding ditches filled with water, stood next to the factory, with four hundred British police officers guarding them. When the first wave of demonstrators reached the Salt Works, police ran toward the protesters and began to bash them with five-foot-long steel-tipped clubs. The demonstrators were knocked to the ground, but they showed no resistance. The second wave of demonstrators approached; again, the police rushed up and beat them. Bodies covered the ground. But not a single Indian fought back. The police did not know what to do. They finally stopped beating the demonstrators, found Sarojini Naidu, and arrested her. Manilal Gandhi was also placed under arrest.

When Vallabhbhai Patel, the leader of the swaraj movement since Gandhi's arrest, arrived at Dharasana Salt Works, he said,

> All hope of reconciling India with the British Empire is lost forever. I can understand any government's taking people into custody and punishing them for breaches of the law, but I cannot understand how any government that calls itself civilized could deal as savagely and brutally with nonviolent, unresisting men as the British have this morning. [43]

The Dharasana Salt Works demonstration was over.

LONDON

Across India, people were frustrated about India's situation, including Great Britain's viceroy, Lord Irwin. In November 1930, the Round Table Conference (a series of meeting to discuss India's future) began in London. It met for three months to discuss the possibility of dominion status for India. Without any members of the Indian National Congress present at the conference, Irwin reached his limit of tolerance with the British control. He ordered that Gandhi and the other members of the Indian National Congress be released from prison. Gandhi was released in January 1931.

Gandhi and Irwin met in Delhi to discuss India's situation. They agreed to the so-called Gandhi-Irwin Pact, which they signed on March 5, 1931. The pact stated that Gandhi and the Indian National Congress would put an end to civil disobedience and Irwin and the British government would allow those Indians living along the coast to make their own salt. Irwin would also release all *satyagrahis*, or people who practice satyagraha, from prison and arrange for a Second Round Table Conference, to be held in London. India called on Gandhi to represent the Indian National Congress at the Second Round Table Conference.

After signing the Gandhi-Irwin Pact, Gandhi again spent a great deal of his time listening to the people of India. He would take his spinning wheel and sit spinning and listening to people's complaints, worries, and praises. Gandhi assured the people that their relatives would be released from jail, and that the fight for swaraj would continue.

Gandhi, along with his youngest son, Devadas, and numerous friends, set sail for England from Bombay. Once in England, Gandhi kept himself very busy, often getting only a few hours of sleep a night. In addition to attending the conference, Gandhi made a point of visiting the poor areas of the nation and talking to the unemployed and to the mill workers. The cotton workers in Lancashire were especially happy to speak with him. They appreciated his insight and were impressed with his knowledge of the cotton industry. Gandhi suggested that with India's independence, Great Britain and India could resume the former cotton trade, which would create jobs for a great number of unemployed British. The mill workers liked the idea.

The Second Round Table Conference, however, did not go as smoothly as the informal talks with the mill workers. The British were not ready to grant independence to India. The Hindus, Muslims, Untouchables, and other minority groups spent most of the conference bickering among themselves. The British used this to their advantage. As long as the Indians couldn't agree on how to run an independent India, Great Britain could claim that it was useless to put forth a proposal for independence.

When the Second Round Table Conference closed, India was no closer to obtaining independence than before the meeting began. The Indian representatives from various groups had failed to unite for the good of their country. Gandhi was deeply humiliated and felt personally responsible for the failure of the conference.

FASTING IN PRISON

Gandhi returned to India on December 28, 1931, to find a new viceroy, Lord Willingdon, in charge. He also found that civil disobedience had returned to India. Lord Willingdon arrested Gandhi on January 4, 1932, and put him back in Yeravda Prison. Soon to follow were the rest of the leaders of Congress. In fact, more than thirty thousand Indian politicians were put in prison within two months. Yet again, Gandhi took to prison life by spinning, praying, and reading.

While in prison, Gandhi learned that the British government was planning to hold separate elections to allow the Untouchables to vote for their own representatives. For other elections, the Untouchables would vote with the Hindus. Muslims and other groups would have their own elections. Gandhi was appalled at this plan. He had fought long and hard for the unity of India's people, including the Untouchables, and did not want to see them separated from the rest of the people. Gandhi had once said, "I regard untouchability as the greatest blot on Hinduism." [44] As a result, Gandhi declared that he would "fast unto death" against separate elections for the Untouchables.

On September 20, Gandhi woke and said his morning prayer. He ate his breakfast of milk and fruit and then, in the late morning, took his last meal: lemon juice and honey with hot water. Gandhi's fast began. The mahatma, now nearly sixty-three years old, was much older than he had been during his twenty-one-day fast in Delhi in 1924. He had also made a point of drinking a small sip of water every hour during his Delhi fast. This time,

BUCKINGHAM PALACE

During Gandhi's stay in London, he visited Buckingham Palace. Here, he had tea with King George V, whose coronation had taken place in 1911. At that time, Gandhi had supported the British Empire. Now, twenty years later, the situation had changed between King George V and Gandhi. They no longer saw eye-to-eye. When they spoke about the purpose of Gandhi's trip to England, the king advised Gandhi not to stir up trouble.

When Gandhi arrived at the castle, some Britons took issue with Gandhi's appearance—his simple dhoti and shawl. They believed that, while visiting the king, Gandhi should have worn English apparel, like the fine suits he had worn while attending school in London. Gandhi felt differently. Commenting on the Britons' attitude toward Gandhi's clothes, biographer William Shirer wrote: "A few Britons regarded this as showing a lack of respect for the sovereign. But Gandhi took it all lightheartedly. Asked by an English reporter if he thought his loincloth was 'appropriate' for Buckingham Palace, where formal dress was required, Gandhi quipped: 'The King was wearing enough for us both.'"*

Gandhi had not set aside his principles for what the public deemed "appropriate." Khadi was a symbol of India's fight for independence. Gandhi's traditional Indian clothing, which was made out of the fabric representing this freedom, symbolized his commitment to India's struggle for independence.

Source: William L. Shirer, *Gandhi: A Memoir*, New York: A Touchstone Book, Simon & Schuster, 1979, p. 166.

there was no preset end to the fast, so he took the water sips with less precision. He quickly lost his energy and was unable to walk. Nurses attended him around the clock. His only nourishment was an occasional sip of soda water.

Two days after Gandhi began his fast, Kasturbai was permitted to join her husband in prison, to help look after him. Six days after beginning his fast, Gandhi learned that a new proposal, called the Yeravda Pact, had been approved by the London Cabinet. The pact eliminated separate elections for the Untouchables. Kasturbai handed Gandhi a glass of orange juice, and he took a drink, breaking his six-day fast in a ceremony held at Yeravda Prison.

HARIJANS

Gandhi began to use the name *Harijans,* meaning "Children of God," to refer to the Untouchables. Although the Harijans still faced discrimination, their lives improved following Gandhi's Yeravda fast. Hundreds of Hindu temples opened their doors for the first time to Harijans. Biographer Louis Fischer wrote,

> after the fast, untouchability forfeited its public approval, the belief in it was destroyed. . . . It had been socially improper to consort with Harijans; in many circles now it became socially improper not to consort with them. To practice untouchability branded one a bigot, a reactionary. Before long, marriages were taking place between Harijans and Hindus; Gandhi made a point of attending some.[45]

Although these dramatic changes took place soon after Gandhi broke his fast, the three-thousand-year-old stigma of "Untouchability" was not so easily cast aside. Intolerant attitudes and actions toward Harijans still existed throughout India.

In February 1933, Gandhi founded another newspaper, this one entitled *Harijan.* In it, Gandhi voiced his opinions about Untouchability. Six months later, Gandhi was released from prison. Then, in November 1933, he and Kasturbai began a twelve-thousand-mile, nine-month journey across India to speak out against discrimination against Harijans. As the Gandhis traveled across the country, they stopped to talk to the peasants in countless villages. Some Hindus resented Gandhi's desire to end Untouchability. At the end of the trip, Gandhi and Kasturbai were nearly hit by a bomb that had been thrown at their procession of cars. The bomb hit the first car; Gandhi and his wife had been riding in the second. Seven people were injured as a result of the bomb. Gandhi had narrowly missed assassination.

A SLOWER PACE

After Gandhi's extensive tour, he was in need of rest. At the end of 1934, he stopped his involvement in the Indian National Congress. During the next two years, Gandhi worked with rural Indian villages, helping to teach peasants the importance of proper sanitation, simple living, and self-reliance. Biographer William Shirer noted how Gandhi

> . . . exhorted the illiterate villagers to educate their children, clean up their filthy streets and backyards, stop defecating in them and build proper latrines, purify their drinking water . . . learn how to breed cattle and fertilize their fields, take up spinning and weaving to clothe themselves properly . . . establish co-ops to market their produce and buy what they needed . . . practice toleration of other faiths, do away with untouchability . . . and, above all, discover that in themselves and in their cooperative efforts lay their salvation. [46]

Years earlier, in 1908, Gandhi wrote *Hind Swaraj* (*"Indian Home Rule"*), a pamphlet published in 1909. Gandhi said of the pamphlet, "In my opinion it is a book which can be put into the hands of a child. It teaches the gospel of love in place of that of hate. It replaces violence with self-sacrifice. It pits soul force against brute force." [47] In it, he wrote about his dislike for modern civilization and his desire to return to traditional ways of life. During Gandhi's work with Indian villagers in the 1930s, he put these ideas into action, teaching the villagers how to plow their lands and how to spin.

In 1936, Gandhi took up residence in Sevagram Ashram, located in central India near Wardha. The ashram was secluded and living conditions there were meager. The residents, who included Gandhi and a few of his followers, lived in a single twenty-nine-by-fourteen-foot hut made of mud-brick walls and a thatched roof. Gandhi spent his time spinning, talking with the nearby villagers, mostly Harijans; writing for *Harijan*; and reading. Kasturbai joined him at Sevagram Ashram, but found the living conditions difficult. Eventually, ashram members built her a special house, because she could not get accustomed to the lack of privacy. As the ashram grew, the residents built additional huts to accommodate new members.

As Gandhi fell into his life of visiting rural villages and working to improve their medical facilities, education, and sanitation, he was also aware of a new political threat in Europe—Adolf Hitler. Soon Gandhi would find himself back in the thick of trying to rid India of British rule.

WORLD WAR II

Adolf Hitler was the founder of the National Socialist Workers' Party, also called the Nazi Party. In 1933, Hitler had made himself dictator of Germany and was using violence and force to control the nation. Gandhi defined Hitler's tactics as "naked, ruthless force reduced to an exact science and worked with scientific precision." [48]

From the Sevagram Ashram in India, Gandhi read about Hitler's actions and became increasingly worried. Hitler believed that the Germans were a superior race and he was working to wipe out other peoples he considered "inferior"— especially the Jewish population. Gandhi had numerous close Jewish friends. He wrote about the Jews in *Harijan*: "My sympathies are all with the Jews. I have known them intimately in South Africa. Some of them became lifelong companions. Through these friends I came to learn much of their age-long persecution. They have been the Untouchables of Christianity.

The parallel between their treatment by Christians and the treatment of Untouchables by Hindus is very close."[49]

On September 1, 1939, the Nazis invaded Poland; two days later, Great Britain and France declared war on Germany. World War II had begun. The war began with Germany, Italy, and Japan (the three major Axis powers) fighting England and France (known as the Allies).

Not quite a year later, on June 16, 1940, Germany occupied France. At this time, Hitler and his Nazi Party controlled almost all of Western Europe. Great Britain was on its own. Hitler began an air war over England. From August 1940 until October 1941, German planes continually dropped bombs on London. Despite the force of the German onslaught, the British lost only nine hundred planes compared with the twenty-three hundred planes the Germans lost. Defeated, Hitler stopped the air war. Then, on December 7, 1941, Japan attacked the U.S. naval base at Pearl Harbor, Hawaii; this act brought the United States into the conflict, making the war global. Japan then turned its attention to occupying India.

India was already involved in the war, since Great Britain had included it when the British declared war on Germany. The Indian National Congress had not been pleased. Many of its members argued that Indians should only aid the war effort if they were given complete independence from Great Britain. Gandhi felt differently. In an article for *Young India*, he wrote: "if there ever could be a justifiable war in the name of and for humanity, war against Germany to prevent the wanton persecution of a whole race would be completely justified. But . . . I do not believe in any war."[50] In late 1941 and early 1942, Gandhi campaigned against the war.

As it became more apparent that Japan was going to attack India, Britain realized it would need India's support to fight Japan. In March 1942, the British government sent Sir Stafford Cripps to India. Cripps was a member of the British War Cabinet and he brought with him a set of proposals for Indian leaders to consider. The proposals stated that India would receive dominion status at the close of World War II in return for the Indians' help in the war against the Japanese. The proposals contained a catch, however. Following the war, independent states, provinces, and religious minorities would have the option of making their own settlement with the British. This would mean that any one group—be it a state, province, or religious minority—could become its own independent country. There would no longer be an "India" as it currently existed. Gandhi told Cripps: "You are proposing . . . perpetual vivisection of India."[51] India rejected Great Britain's proposals.

QUIT INDIA

After Cripps returned to England, Gandhi stated, "I want freedom immediately . . . this very night—before dawn, if it can be had. . . . Do or die! We shall either free India or die in the attempt. We shall not live to see the perpetuation of our slavery."[52] Gandhi called the campaign to force out Great Britain "Quit India." It was set to begin on August 8, 1942. But before he could launch the movement, the government sprang into action to arrest Mahatma Gandhi.

Gandhi, along with his secretary Mahadev Desai, his chief aide Sarojini Naidu, and all the leaders of the Indian National Congress, including Jawaharlal Nehru, were arrested and imprisoned at Aga Khan Palace, located near Yeravda Prison in Poona. The day after Gandhi's arrest, Kasturbai, too, was arrested after British officials found out she was planning to make one of Gandhi's speeches for him. She joined the others held at Aga Khan.

Just days after his arrest, Mahadev Desai died of a heart attack in prison. Gandhi was deeply upset by his death, as Desai had been a loyal secretary for more than twenty years.

After Gandhi's arrest, unrest took over India. Indians set fire to British government buildings and attacked British officials. Gandhi was now seventy-three years old. He had spent most of his life fighting for the rights of Indians and the freedom of his country through satyagraha. Now behind bars once again, he watched his beloved India turn to violence. British Viceroy Lord Linlithgow blamed Gandhi for the unrest, while Gandhi blamed it on his arrest by the viceroy. Gandhi declared that he would begin a twenty-one-day fast.

9

Independence
at Last

*We are aiming at a world federation in which
India would be a leading unit. It can come
only through non-violence.*

—Mohandas Gandhi

To protect against the horrific violence spreading across India, Mahatma Gandhi began a twenty-one-day fast on February 9, 1943. His body was not in especially good shape even at the beginning of the fast, due to his lifelong habit of undertaking occasional fasts and his limited diet. With nine doctors caring for him, as well as Kasturbai and Sarojini Naidu, Gandhi managed to survive the fast—but just barely. When doctors examined Gandhi on March 2, 1943, they concluded that he had malaria, hookworm, amoebic dysentery, and acute anemia.

KASTURBAI'S DEATH AND CREMATION

One year after his fast, while still in prison, Gandhi was faced with a tragic event. On February 22, 1944, his wife, Kasturbai, died. She had been ill with bronchitis and pneumonia for several months. Doctors had recommended that she be given an injection of penicillin, but Gandhi had not wanted her to be exposed to injections, which he viewed as violent.

In Kasturbai's final hours, she was with those she loved. Gandhi spent time comforting and holding her. Her youngest son, Devadas, cared for her and spoke to her. She also had numerous nurses and doctors tending to her needs. Right before she died, she called for Gandhi, who came to her bedside and held her in his arms. Devadas described the final minutes:

> As I stood in front watching along with ten others I saw that the shadow on mother's face had deepened; but she spoke and moved her arms about for fuller comfort. . . . Then in the twinkling of an eye the collapse came. Tears rolled down from several eyes while Gandhiji forced back his. The entire group stood in a semi-circle and chanted the favorite prayer which they had been used to say so long in her company. Within minutes she was still. . . .[53]

Gandhi's reaction to Kasturbai's death was one of profound sadness and he became depressed. Gandhi and Kasturbai had been married for sixty-two years. They had grown up and grown old together. Biographer Judith Brown wrote, "He felt her death deeply, far more than he thought he would on his own admission. Thereafter he paid tribute to her courage and faithfulness through all the strangeness of the life to which he had introduced her."[54]

Kasturbai's body was cremated the next day, on February 23, near the palace in which she had been incarcerated. Kasturbai's body looked peaceful; she was dressed in a white khadi sari. Kasturbai's sons carried the *bier*, the stand on which the corpse was placed, from Aga Khan Palace to the place of cremation. A Brahmin priest conducted the short, simple funeral ceremony.

Gandhi watched the ceremony without showing outward emotion, except when Kasturbai's bier was placed on the pyre. At that moment, Gandhi used his shawl to wipe his eyes. Then he performed a short service, which included readings from the Koran, the Bhagavad Gita, and the Bible. Following Gandhi's service, the priest performed the last stages of the ceremony. Sandalwood was placed on top of Kasturbai's body. Devadas lit the pyre as he circled it three times. Kasturbai's body was engulfed in flames and reduced to ashes.

END OF WORLD WAR II

Gandhi spent three more months in prison after his wife's death. Including both South Africa and India, Gandhi had spent six and a half years in prison; his incarceration in Aga Khan Palace would be his last. Gandhi was released on May 6, 1944, due to his increasingly poor health. His body was weak; it took him months to recuperate. Once Gandhi did recover, however, he turned again to politics.

On his release from prison, Gandhi learned that Great Britain had no intention of granting independence to India prior to the end of World War II. In addition, Britain wanted assurance from Hindus and Muslims that they could agree on how to run a government for an independent India together. Prominent Muslim leader Muhammad Ali Jinnah had other ideas. He did not like the fact that the Muslim community of India was much smaller than the Hindu community. He worried that the Muslims' fate would forever be in the hands of the Hindus. To remedy this, he wanted to see a separate all-Muslim state called Pakistan, with himself as the ruler.

Gandhi disagreed with Jinnah and felt there was no reason that Hindus and Muslims could not live together peacefully. He did not want to see India torn apart. He decided to embark on a campaign to build Hindu-Muslim unity. To do so, he first asked Muhammad Ali Jinnah to meet with him to discuss the situation. Gandhi and Jinnah met fourteen times, between September 9 and September 27, 1944, at Jinnah's home in Bombay. The meetings were unsuccessful. Neither leader would budge from his viewpoint.

World War II ended on September 2, 1945, when Japan officially surrendered; Germany had surrendered four months earlier, on May 8. Before Great Britain would grant India its independence, though, it insisted that the Hindus and Muslims work out their disagreement. As a result of the growing tensions between Hindus, Muslims, and the British, riots began to break out across India.

THE FINAL BATTLE

In 1946 and 1947, Gandhi traveled across India, pleading with the people to follow satyagraha instead of resorting to violence. Thousands of Indians, both Hindus and Muslims, died as a result of the riots.

On August 16, 1946, riots in Calcutta left at least five thousand Indians dead. In October of the same year, Muslims began mass killings of Hindus in Noakhali, located in the northeast province of Bengal. Gandhi spent nearly four months, from November 7, 1946, to March 2, 1947, in Noakhali trying to establish peace between the Hindus and Muslims there. In a speech he made on November 10, 1946, Gandhi said, "Whether you believe me or not, I want to assure you that I am a servant of both the Hindus and the Mussalmans [Muslims]. I have not come here to fight Pakistan. If India is destined to be partitioned, I cannot prevent it. But I wish to tell you that Pakistan cannot be established by force."[55] Throughout Gandhi's time spent in Noakhali, he emphasized the importance of nonviolence and unity.

MUHAMMAD ALI JINNAH

In their early years, Muhammad Ali Jinnah and Mohandas Gandhi both appeared to have the same common goals: to gain independence from Great Britain and to bring unity to the Hindu and Muslim communities. Both men had grown up in the same area in India (although Jinnah was six years younger than Gandhi) and both had traveled to England to study law. They had both started out with a tolerance for all religions. At one time, like Gandhi, Jinnah was a member of the Indian National Congress.

Over time, however, Jinnah's goals changed. Muslims made up about one-quarter of India's total population. Jinnah worried that, in an independent India, the Muslims would not have a strong enough voice. He officially withdrew from the Indian National Congress, although he did work with Congress on specific decision-making policies. He focused all his efforts on obtaining a separate country for Muslims—one called Pakistan.

In addition to different political views, Jinnah also held values and beliefs that were different from Gandhi's. Jinnah had become a wealthy lawyer and politician, leader of the Muslim League. He lived on a large estate in Bombay. He enjoyed fine wine, expensive food, and Western clothes. When he traveled, he always went first-class and stayed in the most extravagant hotels. He disagreed with Gandhi's belief about accepting the Untouchables. Jinnah felt bitterness toward the Untouchables and wanted nothing to do with them. He felt the Untouchables should have no position in an independent India's government; only the wealthy and well-educated should have a say in running the nation.

As Jinnah's values and beliefs began to contrast so drastically with Gandhi's, Jinnah came to dislike the Mahatma. Jinnah told an interviewer, "I hate all this Hindu nonsense about cows being sacred and the Hindus telling us that we Moslems have no right to kill them for beef. . . . I resent a Hindu feeling it's unclean to eat with me, a Moslem, or even to shake my hand. Of course, Gandhi doesn't go that far, I admit, but he has his Hindu peculiarities."*

Source: William L. Shirer, *Gandhi: A Memoir*, New York: A Touchstone Book, Simon & Schuster, 1979, p. 120.

In March 1947, Hindus in the state of Bihar began mass killings of Muslims. Gandhi left Noakhali and traveled to Bihar, where he again spoke out for peace between Hindus and Muslims. His words fell on deaf ears.

On March 22, 1947, a new British viceroy, Louis Mountbatten, arrived in India to officially grant it independence from Great Britain. He had been sent by British Prime Minister Clement Atlee, who had stated that India would gain independence no later than June 1948. Mountbatten's task would be difficult, as the Hindus and Muslims did not seem close to coming to an agreement as to how to run the government of a new, free India.

In fact, Mountbatten found that Jinnah was unwilling to consider anything but a country of their own for the Muslims. Mountbatten did, however, find most of the other members of the Indian National Congress more willing to negotiate. Jawaharlal Nehru and Vallabhbhai Patel both agreed that a free, but divided, India was better than an India under British rule. They were willing to give Pakistan to Jinnah and the Muslims. Gandhi, on the other hand, refused to agree to the deal. To Mountbatten he said, "You'll have to divide my body before you divide India."[56] Not a single other Congress member sided with Gandhi. He confided to one of his aides, "I find myself alone. . . . Even Patel and Nehru think I'm wrong. . . . They wonder if I have not deteriorated with age. Maybe they are right and I alone am floundering in darkness."[57]

A FREE INDIA

Two years after the end of World War II, on August 15, 1947, the goal Mahatma Gandhi had worked so long to achieve finally happened: India was granted independence from Great Britain. Jawaharlal Nehru was named its first prime minister. Yet India's independence did not bring the happiness Gandhi had envisioned. He had wanted a united independent India, with Hindus and Muslims living and working together; what he got was a divided independent India, with Hindus making up the country called India, and Muslims living in a separate country called Pakistan.

Gandhi was seventy-seven years old at the time that swaraj was granted. His body was weak and he was beginning to feel the effects of his frequent fasts and sparse diet. He had survived much of his life on little sleep—always opting to take on the extra meeting in hopes of helping a cause. Gandhi was worn out.

Celebrations for a free India began on the day after Prime Minister Nehru's proclamation of India's independence. A country now totaling some 350 million people rejoiced with Independence Day celebrations. Gandhi did not participate. He spent the day praying and stayed away from the public eye.

Gandhi was horrified at the bloodshed he witnessed in the new, free India. William Shirer wrote: "All his lifelong teaching and practice of non-violence, which had been so successful in the struggle against the British, had come to naught. The realization that it had failed to keep his fellow Indians from flying at one another's throats the moment they were free from the British shattered him."[58]

In Calcutta at the end of August 1947, Gandhi was in the midst of terrible fighting among the Hindus and Muslims. After seeing the bodies lying in the streets, and the buildings and temples swallowed up by flames, he announced that he was going to begin a fast. He vowed not to eat again until the Hindus and Muslims agreed to stop the violence. He added, "Let all understand that a make-believe peace cannot satisfy me. I do not want a temporary lull to be followed by worse conflagration. In that event I shall have to go on an unconditional fast unto death."[59] Gandhi began his fast on September 2, 1947, and continued for three days. He broke his fast on September 4, after prominent members of the Hindu and Muslim communities assured Gandhi that they would end the violence.

Following this fast, Gandhi traveled to Delhi. Once there, Vallabhbhai Patel quickly moved Gandhi into the home of G.D. Birla, who had been a longtime supporter of Gandhi's. Birla had offered Gandhi financial support and campaigned for Gandhi's causes. Birla was one of the wealthiest industrialists in India. He had a huge estate surrounded by a stone wall. His home, Patel reasoned, would offer Gandhi a safe place in which to live.

In the city of Delhi, Gandhi was shocked by what he found. The killings stopped once Gandhi had arrived; his mere presence had made that happen. But thick tension remained. And wherever Gandhi traveled, he ran into more dead bodies, more charred buildings—and everywhere, more frightened people.

Gandhi declared another fast, which would be his last, scheduled to begin on January 13, 1948. The Mahatma's already weak body could scarcely handle the strain. He was losing two pounds a day. Within a few days, he was nearly in a coma. Hindu and Muslim leaders worked quickly to put together a written agreement that declared peace between them. On January 18, after all of the Delhi leaders had signed the agreement, Gandhi broke his fast.

Not all Indians were happy, however. Some Hindu extremists felt that Gandhi's insistence on accepting Muslims was a betrayal of the Hindu community. They believed Gandhi should have died in his final fast. A few of them, including a man named Nathuram Godse, decided to kill Gandhi themselves. They made an unsuccessful attempt on January 20, setting off a bomb during Gandhi's evening prayers in the Birla House gardens. No one was hurt. The next time, however, would be different.

10

Never
Forgotten

*Peace will not come out of a clash of arms but
out of justice lived and done by unarmed nations
in the face of odds.*

—Mohandas Gandhi

On January 30, 1948, Gandhi ate dinner in the company of Vallabhbhai Patel. Dining in the Birla House, they discussed differences Patel had been having with Jawaharlal Nehru. Time was running short, however, and Gandhi told Patel he had to leave in order to lead an evening prayer meeting, to be held alongside the grounds' gardens.

Running late, which he did not like, Gandhi walked to the prayer meeting with the help of his grandnieces, Manubehn and Abhabehn. He used their shoulders for support, as his body was still greatly weakened from his last fast. As he approached the platform on which he would say the prayer, he heard someone cry, "*Bapuji! Bapuji!* (Father! Father!)" Gandhi turned to see a Hindu man approaching him. The man bowed his head, pulled out a black Beretta, and shot Gandhi three times in the chest. After the shots, Gandhi fell to the ground, his head cradled in Manubehn and Abhabehn's arms. Gandhi's final words were, "*Hey, Rama* (Oh, God)." Within minutes, Mahatma Gandhi was dead.

The police captured Gandhi's killer, Hindu extremist Nathuram Godse, on the same evening of the assassination. Godse was a young journalist from the city of Poona and a member of the highest Hindu caste, a Brahmin. He resented Gandhi's actions in trying to unite Hindus and Muslims. Godse felt that Hindus were better than Muslims. At his trial, Godse was sentenced to death.

Gandhi's sons tried to have the sentence changed, since they knew that their father would not want his murderer killed—that would violate everything Gandhi had stood for. Despite their efforts, Godse was hanged on November 15, 1949, in the courtyard of Ambala Prison.

MAHATMA GANDHI KI JAI ("LONG LIVE MAHATMA GANDHI")

The news of Gandhi's assassination on January 30, 1948, spread quickly. All-India Radio broadcast the news within the hour of his death. The new nation was in shock. Jawaharlal Nehru addressed the country that evening. In a speech that emphasized the fact that Gandhi's killer had been a Hindu (in the hope of preventing a violent backlash against Muslims), he said:

> Friends and comrades, the light has gone out of our lives and there is darkness everywhere. . . . Our beloved leader, Bapu as we called him, the father of the nation, is no more. The light has gone out, I said, and yet I was wrong. . . . For that light represented something more than the immediate present; it represented the living truth, the eternal truths, reminding us of the right path, drawing us from error, taking this ancient country to freedom.[60]

Hindus and Muslims alike mourned Mahatma Gandhi's death. The violence in India, which had escalated since its independence, suddenly dropped. A Muslim politician wrote, "His assassination had a cathartic effect and throughout India men realized with a shock the depth to which hatred and discord had dragged them. The Indian nation turned back from the brink of the abyss and millions blessed the memory of the man who had made redemption possible."[61] For the time being, India was at peace, as people showed their respects to a man whose fondest wish had been to see his country free and living in truth and love.

The next day, on January 31, Mahatma Gandhi's funeral march took place. He had specified, before he died, that he did not want his body preserved, but instead wanted a traditional Hindu cremation. Gandhi's body was placed upon a flower-covered military weapons carrier, which was pulled, using ropes, by two hundred men from the Indian Army, Navy, and Air Force. The vehicle's engine was left off. It took four and a half hours for the procession to cover five and a half miles, beginning at the Birla House and proceeding to the banks of Jumna River.

As Gandhi's body was pulled through the masses of Indians, people shouted, "*Mahatma Gandhi Ki Jai!* ("Long Live Mahatma Gandhi!")" From the sky, planes dropped flower petals over the crowds of people, who totaled 1.5 million. The body was taken to the cremation grounds, near Jumna River. The funeral pyre had

MOHANDAS
GANDHI

Although he was condemned by some members of his Hindu faith for leaving India, young Mohandas Gandhi traveled abroad to England to study law. He is seen here in an 1887 photograph.

When they were still children, Mohandas Gandhi married Kasturbai Makanji. Such child marriages, arranged by the parents of the bride and groom, were very common in India in the late nineteenth century when Gandhi came of age. The Gandhis are seen here in a photograph taken around 1915.

During his early years as a lawyer, Gandhi moved to South Africa to help promote the rights of Indians living under British rule in that nation. Seen here in a 1902 photograph, Gandhi (center) is surrounded by fellow workers at his law office in Johannesburg, South Africa.

Upon his return to India from South Africa, Gandhi knew he wanted to work to help the Indian people receive better treatment from their British rulers. Before getting involved directly in political action, though, Gandhi spent a good deal of time studying the people and culture of India, to reacquaint himself with his homeland. During this time, he became even more devoted to his Hindu faith. Seen here is an extraordinary example of Hindu architecture: Kesava Temple in Somnathpur, India, dedicated to the god Vishnu, is known for its beautiful carvings.

One of Gandhi's most successful campaigns was his promotion of Indian self-sufficiency, particularly in regard to textile manufacture. Rather than buy British-made goods, Gandhi began to spin his own cotton cloth (as he is doing in this photograph) in the traditional Indian manner and encouraged his fellow Indians to boycott British cloth.

This photograph taken in Ahmedabad, India, in 1990 shows two of the most significant symbols of Gandhi's life: beautiful native-made Indian cloth being set out to dry in the sun and, resting in the background, the cattle that are considered sacred animals to Hindus.

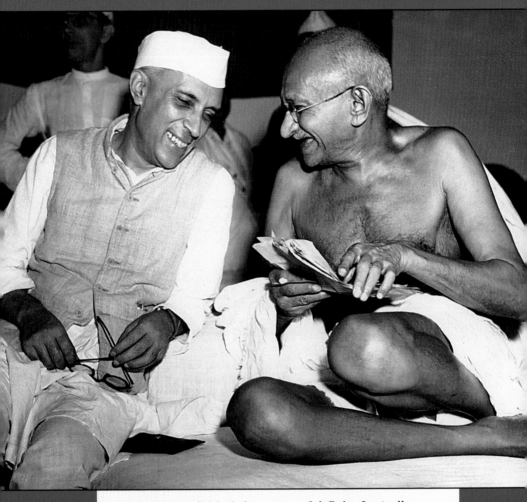

Although Gandhi led the successful fight for Indian independence from Great Britain, he did not become its political leader. That honor went to one of his most devoted friends and followers, Jawaharlal Nehru (seen with Gandhi, at left), who became the first prime minister of the newly independent India.

Despite his constant pleas for peace and nonviolence, Gandhi met his own end at the hands of a radical Hindu assassin. His legacy of passive resistance and spiritual devotion has lived on, however. Thousands of people continue to read his works and visit his tomb (seen here) every year.

been made of stone, brick, and earth, and had been covered with sandalwood logs. When Gandhi's body was placed on the pyre, his head pointed north and his feet south. This symbolic positioning of the body was also used for the Buddha's cremation.

Gandhi's sons watched the ceremony. Ramdas, the Mahatma's third son, lit the funeral pyre. It burned for fourteen hours. Onlookers sang prayers and someone read the entire text of the Bhagavad Gita. The next day, relatives and friends held a second service at which the ashes were collected and placed into a bag made from khadi. The bag was then placed in a copper urn. After thirteen days of mourning, on February 12, 1948, Gandhi's ashes were sprinkled into the seven sacred rivers of India and elsewhere.

TOUCHING THE LIVES OF PEOPLE ACROSS THE WORLD

Gandhi's life and philosophy were well known throughout the world. He touched the lives of many different people—from the poor and unknown to the rich and famous. As people learned about Gandhi's life and what he stood for, some began to embrace his philosophy and ideas and put them into action. In this way, Gandhi lived on, and will continue to live on in the future, in the hearts of millions.

In the 1950s, in the United States, a man named Martin Luther King, Jr., studied Gandhi's writings. He wanted to learn about satyagraha and the methods Gandhi used to obtain Indian freedom. At the time, King was a college student; he later went on to become an internationally known African-American civil rights leader. King found that Gandhi's philosophy fit with his own ideas about nonviolence. King wrote, "For Gandhi, love was a potent instrument for social and collective transformation. It was in this Gandhian emphasis on love and nonviolence that I discovered the method for social reform that I had been seeking for so many months. . . . I came to feel that this was the only morally and practically sound method open to oppressed people in their struggle for freedom."[62]

In South Africa, former President Nelson Mandela was also greatly influenced by Mahatma Gandhi's philosophy. Mandela made a speech in 1997 in which he said,

> Gandhi's magnificent example of personal sacrifice and dedication in the face of oppression was one of his many legacies to our country and to the world. He showed us that it was necessary to brave imprisonment if truth and justice were to triumph over evil. The values of tolerance, mutual respect and unity for which he stood and acted had a profound influence on our liberation movement, and on my own thinking. They inspire us today in our efforts of reconciliation and nation-building. [63]

A MAN REMEMBERED

Gandhi did not live a life without faults or critics. It took much work for him to establish a good relationship with his wife, and he never had an especially close relationship with any of his sons. Orthodox Hindus criticized his attack on the caste system. Some people disapproved of Gandhi's unwillingness to accept modernization. Still others thought Gandhi's use of satyagraha was unrealistic and overly idealistic. Through these faults and critics, we see what Gandhi had insisted all along: He was human.

Gandhi was most at ease and happiest when he spent time with the poor, the overlooked, and the forgotten. He would squat down in the middle of their grim surroundings and reach out to them. He listened to their concerns and talked to them about how they could improve their lives. He laughed and joked with them and made them feel like they were his equals, as he truly saw them. Prime Minister Jawaharlal Nehru wrote about Gandhi, "He did not descend from the top; he seemed to emerge from the millions of India, speaking their language and incessantly drawing attention to them and their appalling condition. Get off the backs of these peasants and workers, he told us, all you who live by their exploitation; get rid of the system that produces this poverty and misery." [64]

A correspondent from China for *The Saturday Evening Post*, Ed Snow, had spent time with Gandhi on and off since the 1930s. In his early meetings with Gandhi, Snow was not impressed by the leader and even criticized Gandhi's lack of support for the British during World War II. Then, when Snow returned to India in 1948, he had what fellow journalist William Shirer described as a "great awakening." [65] During this time, Snow experienced firsthand India's discrimination and violence, and he came to greatly admire Gandhi's insights and wisdom. After learning of Gandhi's death, Snow wrote, "There was a mirror in the Mahatma in which everyone could see the best in himself, and when the mirror broke, it seemed that the thing in oneself might be fled forever." [66]

Across the world, people continue to celebrate the teachings of Mahatma Gandhi. He taught the world a way of living—through truth and love. He shed light on how people were treated unequally and gave people a way to remedy that injustice—through truth and love. He believed that truth and love were found in tolerance and acceptance of others. In his autobiography, Gandhi wrote, "To see the universal and all-pervading Spirit of Truth face to face one must be able to love the meanest of creation as oneself. And a man who aspires after that cannot afford to keep out of any field of life." [67]

FROM *HIND SWARAJ (INDIAN HOME RULE)*— CHAPTER 1: THE CONGRESS AND ITS OFFICIALS

Reader: Just at present there is a Home Rule wave passing over India. All our countrymen appear to be pining for National Independence. A similar spirit pervades them even in South Africa. Indians seem to be eager to acquire rights, Will you explain your views in this matter?

Editor: You have put the question well, but the answer is not easy. One of the objects of a newspaper is to understand popular feeling and to give expression to it, another is to arouse among the people certain desirable sentiments, and the third is fearlessly to expose popular defects. The exercise of all these three functions is involved in answering your question. To a certain extent the people's will has to be expressed, certain sentiments will need to be fostered, and defects will have to be brought to light. But, as you have asked the question, it is my duty to answer it.

Reader: Do you then consider that a desire for Home Rule has been created among us?

Editor: That desire gave rise to the National Congress. The choice of the word "National" implies it.

Reader: That surely, is not the case. *Young India* seems to ignore the Congress. It is considered to be an instrument for perpetuating British Rule.

Editor: That opinion is not justified. Had not the Grand Old Man of India prepared the soil, our young men could not have even spoken about Home Rule. How can we forget what Mr. Hume has written, how he has lashed us into action, and with what effort he has awakened us, in order to achieve the objects of the Congress?

Sir William Wedderburn has given his body, mind and money to the same cause. His writings are worthy of perusal to this day. Professor Gokhale in order to prepare the nation, embraced poverty and gave twenty years of his life. Even now, he is living in poverty. The late Justice Budruddin Tyebji was also one of those who, through the Congress, sowed the seed of Home Rule. Similarly, in Bengal, Madras, the Punjab and other places, there have been lovers of India and members of the Congress, both Indian and English.

Reader: Stay, stay, you are going too far, you are straying away from my question. I have asked you about Home or Self-Rule; you are discussing foreign rule. I do not desire to bear English names, and you are giving me such names. In these circumstances, I do not think we can ever meet. I shall be pleased if you will confine yourself to Home Rule. All other talk will not satisfy me.

Editor: You are impatient. I cannot afford to be likewise. If you will bear with me for a while. I think you will find that you will obtain what you want. Remember the old proverb that the tree does not grow in one day. The fact that you have checked me and that you do not want to bear about the well-wishers of India shows that, for you at any rate, Home Rule is yet far away. If we had many like you, we would never make any advance. This thought is worthy of your attention.

Reader: It seems to me that you simply want to put me off by talking round and round. Those whom you consider to be well-wishers of India are not such in my estimation. Why, then, should I listen to your discourse on such people? What has he whom you consider to be the Father of the Nation done for it? He says that the

English Governors will do justice and that we should co-operate with them.

Editor: I must tell you, with all gentleness that it must be a matter of shame for us that you should speak about that great man in terms of disrespect. Just look at his work. He has dedicated his life to the service of India. We have learned what we know from him. It was the respects Dadabbai who taught us that the English had sucked our lifeblood. What does it matter that, today, his trust is still in the English nation! Is Dadabbai less to be honored because, in the exuberance of youth, we are prepared to go a step further? Are we, on that account, wiser than he? It is a mark of wisdom not to kick away the very step from which we have risen higher. The removal of a step from a staircase brings down the whole of it. When, out of infancy, we grow into youth, we do not despise infancy, but, on the contrary, we recall with affection the days of our childhood. If, after many years of study, a teacher were to teach me something, and if I were to build a little more on the foundation laid by that teacher, I would not, on that account, be considered wiser than the teacher. He would always command my respect. Such is the case with the Grand Old Man of India. We must admit that he is the author of nationalism.

Reader: You have spoken well. I can now understand that we must look upon Mr. Dadabhai with respect. Without him and men like him, we should probably not have the spirit that fires us. How can the same be said of Professor Gokhale? He has constituted himself a great friend of the English, he says that we have to learn a great deal from them, that we have to learn their political wisdom, before we can talk of Home Rule. I am tired of reading his speeches.

Editor: If you are tired, it only betrays your impatience. We believe that those, who are discontented with the slowness of their parents and are angry because the parents would not run with their children, are considered disrespectful to their parents. Professor Gokhale occupies the place of a parent. What does it matter if he cannot run with us? A nation that is desirous of securing Home Rule cannot afford to despise its ancestors. We shall become useless, if we lack respect for our elders. Only men with mature thoughts are capable of ruling themselves and not the hasty-tempered. Moreover, how many Indians were there like Professor Gokhale when he gave himself to Indian education? I verify believe that whatever Professor Gokhale does, he does with pure motives and with a view of serving India. His devotion to the Motherland is so great that he would give his life for it, if necessary. Whatever he says is said not to flatter anyone but because he believes it to be true. We are bound, therefore to entertain the highest regard for him.

Reader: Are we, then, to follow him in every respect?

Editor: I never said any such thing. If we conscientiously differed from him, the learned Professor himself would advise us to follow the dictates of our conscience rather than him. Our chief purpose is not to decry his work, but to believe that he is infinitely greater than we are, and to feel assured that compared, with his work for India, ours is infinitesimal. Several newspapers write disrespectfully of him. It is our duty against such writings. We should consider men like Professor Gokhale to be the pillars of Home Rule. It is bad habit to say that another man's thoughts are bad and ours only are good and that those holding different views from ours are the enemies of the country.

Reader: I now begin to understand somewhat your meaning, I shall have to think the matter over. But what you say about Mr. Hume and Sir William Wedderburn is beyond my comprehension.

Editor: The same rule holds good for the English as for the Indians. I can never subscribe to the, statement that all Englishmen are bad. Many Englishmen desire Home Rule for India. That the English people are somewhat more selfish than others is true, but that does not prove that every Englishman is bad. We who seek justice will have to do justice to others. Sir William does not wish ill to India,—that should be enough for us. As we proceed, you will see that, if we act justly India will be sooner free. You will see, too, that if we shun every Englishman as an enemy, Home Rule will be delayed. But if we are just to them, we shall receive their support in our progress towards the goal.

Reader: All this seems to me at present to be simply nonsensical. English support and the obtaining of Home Rule are two contradictory things. How can the English people tolerate Home Rule for us? But I do not want you to decide this question for me just yet. To spend time over it is useless. When you have shown how we can have Home Rule, perhaps I shall understand your views. You have prejudiced against you by discoursing on English help. I would, therefore, beseech you not to continue on this subject.

Editor: I have no desire to do so. That you are prejudiced against me is not a matter for much anxiety. It is well that I should say unpleasant things at the commencement. It is my duty patiently to try to remove your prejudice.

Reader: I like that last statement. It emboldens me to say what I like. One thing still puzzles me. I do not understand how the Congress laid the foundation of Home Rule.

Editor: Let us see. The Congress brought together Indians from different parts of India, and enthused us with the idea of nationality. The government used to look upon it with disfavor. The Congress has always insisted the nation should control revenue and expenditure. it has always desired self-government after Canadian model. Whether we can get it or not, whether we desire it or not, and whether there is not something more desirable, are different questions. All I have to show is that the Congress gave us a foretaste of Home Rule. To deprive it of the honor is not proper, and for us to do so would not only be ungrateful, but retard the fulfillment of our object. To treat the Congress as an institution inimical to our growth as a nation would disable us from using that body.

APPENDIX

GANDHI ON UNTOUCHABILITY, FROM *HARIJAN*, NOVEMBER 2, 1933

Untouchability as at present practised is the greatest blot on Hinduism. It is (with apologies to Sanatanists) against the Shastras. It is against the fundamental principles of humanity, it is against the dictates of reason that a man should, by mere reason of birth, be for ever regarded as an untouchable, even unapproachable and unseeable. These adjectives do not convey the full meaning of the thing itself. It is a crime for certain men, women and their children to touch, or to approach within stated distances, or to be seen by those who are called caste-Hindus. The tragedy is that millions of Hindus believe in this institution as if it was enjoined by the Hindu religion.

Happily, Hindu reformers have recoiled with horror from this practice. They have come to the conclusion that it has no support in the Hindu Shastras taken as a whole. Isolated texts torn from their context and considered by themselves can no doubt be produced in support of this, practice, as of any evil known to mankind, But there is abundant authority in the Shastras to warrant the summary rejection, as being un-Hindu, of anything or any practice that is manifestly against, the fundamental principles of humanity or morality, of *Ahimsa or Satya*.

This movement against untouchability has been daily gathering strength. It was in last September that leading Hindus, claiming to represent the whole of Hindu India, met together and unanimously passed a resolution, condemning untouchability and pledging themselves to abolish it by law if possible during the existing regime, and, failing that, when India had a Parliament of her own.

Among the marks of untouchability to be removed was the prohibition against temple entry by Harijans. In the course of the struggle, it was discovered that the British Courts in India had recognised this evil custom, so much so that certain acts done by untouchables as such came to be offences under the

British Indian Penal Code. Thus, the entry by an untouchable into a Hindu temple would be punishable as a crime under the I.P.C.

Before, therefore, the movement of temple entry can make headway. It has become imperative to have this anomaly removed. It is for this purpose that Sjt. RangaIyer has given notice of two bills to be introduced in the Central Legislature. After ascertaining the opinion of the Provincial Governments, H.E. the Viceroy has sanctioned the introduction of these Bills. But, being private Bills, they have a poor chance of becoming the law of the land, unless the Government and the members of the Assembly refrain from obstructing its consideration. It may be argued that, being pledged to neutrality in matters of religion, the Government are bound to facilitate the passage of the first Bill at any rate, in as much as it merely seeks to undo the effect produced by the decisions of British Indian Courts, and this it does by withdrawing legal recognition from untouchability.

There are practices in various religions professed by the inhabitants of this land whose breach is not regarded as criminal, though it would be regarded as very serious by the respective religious codes. Thus, beef eating by a Hindu is an offence in the eye of the Hindu religious code, but rightly not punishable as a crime under the Indian Penal Code. Is there, then, any reason why the common law of India should punish a breach of the custom of untouchability? If there are many Hindus learning in the Hindu scriptures who find support in them for the present practice of untouchability, there are quite a number of equally learned Hindus holding the opposite view. Though this opinion of the Pundits has already appeared in the press, it is reproduced elsewhere for ready reference. Let it be noted that the signatories are all orthodox Hindus, as much lovers of their faith as are the learned men of the opposite school. On the 25th of January 1933 was held the session of the All-India Sanatan Dharma Sabha, presided over by Pundit Malaviyaji and attended by over one hundred learned men. It passed a resolution to the effect that Harijans were as much entitled to temple entry as the rest of Hindus.

If the bills are not passed, it is obvious that, the central part of the reform will be hung up almost indefinitely. Neutrality in matters of religion, ought not to mean religious stagnation and hindrance to reform.

With due regard to the Sanatanists, it is difficult to understand the cry of 'religion in danger'. Under neither bill will a single temple be opened against the will of the majority of temple goers in question. The second bill expressly says so. The first bill takes up a neutral attitude. It does not help a Harijan to force his way into a temple. The reformers do not seek to compel the opponents to their will. They desire, by the fairest means possible, to convert the majority or the minority, as the case may be, to their view of untouchability.

It is said that the Harijans themselves do not want temple entry and that they want only betterment of their economic and political condition. The reformer, too, wants the latter, but he believes that this betterment will be much quicker brought about, if religious equality is attained. The reformer denies that the Harijans do not want temple entry. But it may be that they are so disgusted with caste Hindus and Hindu religion itself as to want nothing from them. They may in sullen discontent choose to remain outside the religious pale. Any penance on the part of caste Hindus may be too late.

Nevertheless the caste Hindus who recognise that untouchability is a blot on Hinduism have to atone for the sin of untouchability. Whether, therefore, Harijans desire temple entry or not, caste Hindus have to open their temples to Harijans, precisely on the same terms as the other Hindus. For a caste Hindu with any sense of honour, temple prohibition is a continuous breach of the Pledge taken at the Bombay meeting of September last. Those, who gave their word to the world and to God that they would have the temples opened for the Harijans, have to sacrifice their all, if need be, for redeeming the pledge. It may be that they did not represent the Hindu mind. They have, then, to own defeat and do the proper penance. Temple entry is the one spiritual act that would constitute the message of freedom to the untouchables and assure them that they are not outcastes before God.

APPENDIX

GANDHI ON VIOLENCE AND NONVIOLENCE, 1938

It seems to me that the united action of the Hindus and the Muslims blinded me to the violence that was lurking in the breasts of many. The English who are trained diplomats and administrators are accustomed to line of least resistance, and when they found that it was more profitable to conciliate a big organization than to crush it by extensive frightfulness, they yielded to the extent that they thought was necessary. It is, however, my conviction that our resistance was predominantly nonviolent in action and will be accepted as such by the future historian. As a seeker of truth and nonviolence, however, I must not be satisfied with mere action if it is not from the heart. I must declare from the house-tops that the nonviolence of those days fell far short of the violence as I have so often defined.

Nonviolent action without the co-operation of the heart and the head cannot produce the intended result. The failure of our imperfect ahimsa is visible to the naked eye. Look at the feud that is going on between Hindus and Muslims. Each is arming for the fight with the other. The violence that we had harboured in our breasts during the non-cooperation is now recoiling upon ourselves. The violent energy that was, generated among the masses, but was kept under cheek in the pursuit of common objective, has now been let-loose and is being used among and against ourselves.

The same phenomenon is discernible, though in a less crude manner, in the dissension among Congressmen themselves and the use of forcible methods that the Congress ministers are obliged to adopt in running the administrations under their charge.

This narrative clearly shows that the atmosphere is surcharged with violence. I hope it also shows that nonviolent mass movement is an impossibility unless the atmosphere is radically changed. To blind one's eyes to the events happening around us is to court disaster. It has been suggested to me that I should declare mass civil disobedience and all internal strife will cease, Hindus and Muslims will compose their differences, Congressmen will forget mutual jealousies and fights for power. My reading of the situation is wholly different. If any mass movement is undertaken at the present moment in the name of nonviolence, it will resolve itself into violence largely unorganized and organized in some cases. It will bring discredit on the Congress, spell disaster for the Congress struggle for independence and bring ruin to many a home. This may be a wholly untrue picture born of my weakness. If so, unless I shed that weakness, I cannot lead a movement which requires great strength and resolution.

But if I cannot find an effective purely nonviolent method, outbreak of violence seems to be a certainty. The people demand self-expression. They are not satisfied with the constructive programme prescribed by me and accepted almost unanimously by the Congress. As I have said before, the imperfect response to the constructive programme is itself proof positive of the skin-deep nature of the nonviolence of Congressmen. . . .

There is a growing consciousness of the terrible autocracy of the majority of the States. I admit my responsibility for the suspension of civil resistance in several States. This has resulted in demoralization both among the people and the Princes. The people have lost nerve and feel that all is lost. The demoralization among the Princes consist in their thinking that now they have nothing to fear from their people, nothing substantial to grant. Both are wrong. The result does not dismay me. In fact I had foretold the possibility of these results when I was discussing with Jaipur workers the advisability of suspending the movement, even though it was well circumscribed with rules and restrictions. The demoralization among the people shows that there was not non-violence in thought and word, and therefore, when the intoxication and excitement of jail-going and the accompanying demonstrations ceased, they thought that the struggle was over. The Princes came to the hasty conclusion that they could safely consolidate their autocracy by adopting summary measures against the resisters and placating the docile element by granting eye-wash reforms.

Both the people and the Princes might have reacted in the right manner—the people by recognizing the correctness of my advice and calmly generating strength and energy by quiet and determined constructive effort, and the Princes by seizing the opportunity, afforded by suspension, of doing justice for the sake of justice and granting reforms that would satisfy the reasonable but advanced section among their people. This could only happen, if they recognized the time-spirit. It is neither too late for the people nor the Princes.

In this connection I may not omit the Paramount Power. There are signs of the Paramount Power repenting of the recent declarations about the freedom to the Princes to grant such reforms to their people as they chose. There are audible whispers that the Princes may not take those declarations literally. It is an open secret that the Princes dare not do anything that they guess is likely to displease the Paramount Power. They may not even meet persons whom the Paramount Power may not like them to meet. When there is this tremendous influence exercised over the Princes, it is but natural to hold the Paramount Power responsible for the unadulterated autocracy that reigns supreme in many States.

So, if violence breaks out in this unfortunate land, the responsibility will have to be shared by the Paramount Power, the Princes, and above all by Congressmen. The first two have never claimed to be nonviolent. Their power is frankly derived from and based on the use of violence. But the Congress has since 1920 adopted nonviolence as its settled policy and has undoubtedly striven to act up to it. But as Congressmen never had nonviolence in their hearts, they must reap the fruit of the defect, however unintentional it was. At the crucial moment the defect has come to the surface and the defective method does not seem to meet the situation. Nonviolence is never a method of coercion, it is one of conversion. We have failed to convert the Princes, we have failed to convert the English administrators. It is no use saying that it is impossible to persuade persons willingly to part with their power. I have claimed that Satyagraha is a new experiment. It will be time to pronounce it a failure when Congressmen have given it a genuine trial. Even a policy, if it is honestly pursued, has to be pursued with all one's heart. We have not done so. Hence Congressmen have to convert themselves before the Paramount Power and the Princes can be expected to act justly.

But if the Congressmen can or will go no further than they have done in the direction of nonviolence, and if the Paramount Power and the Princes do not voluntarily and selfishly do the right thing, the country must be prepared for violence, unless the new technique yields a new mode of nonviolent action which will become an effective substitute for violence as a way of securing redress of wrongs. The fact that violence must fail will not prevent its outbreak. Mere constitutional agitation will not do.

APPENDIX

GANDHI'S VIEWS ON GOD AND RELIGION

My own experience has led me to the knowledge that the fullest life is impossible without an immovable belief in a Living Law in obedience to which the whole universe moves. A man without that faith is like a drop thrown out of the ocean bound to perish. Every drop in the ocean shares its majesty and has the honour of giving us the ozone of life.

1. There is an indefinable mysterious power that pervades everything. I feel it, though I do not see it. It is this unseen power that makes itself felt and yet defies proof, because it is so unlike all that I perceive through out the existence of God to a limited extent.

2. I have made the world's faith in God my own, and as my faith is ineffaceable, I regard that to describe faith as experience is to tamper with Truth, it may perhaps be more correct to say that I have no word for characterizing my belief in God.

3. God is that indefinable something which we all feel but which we do not know. To me God is Truth and Love, God is ethics and morality. God is fearlessness, God is the source of light and life and yet. He is above and beyond all these. God is conscience. He is even the atheism of the atheist. He transcends speech and reason. He is a personal God to those who need His touch. He is purest essence. He simply Is to those who have faith. He is long suffering. He is patient but He is also terrible. He is the greatest democrat the world knows. He is the greatest tyrant ever known. We are not, He alone Is.

4. You have asked me why I consider that God is Truth. In my early youth I was taught to repeat what in Hindu scriptures are known as one thousand names of God. But these one thousand names of God were by no means exhaustive. We

believe—and I think it is the truth—that God has as many names as there are creatures and, therefore, we also say that God is nameless and since God has many forms we also consider Him formless, and since He speaks to us through many tongues we consider Him to be speechless and so on. And when I came to study Islam I found that Islam too had many for God. I would say with those who say that God is Love, God is Love. But deep down in me I used to say that thought God may be, God, God is Truth, above all. If it is possible for the human tongue to give the fullest description, I have come to the conclusion that for myself God is Truth. But two years ago, I went a step further and said Truth is God. You will see the fine distinction between the two statements, viz. That God is Truth and Truth is God. And I came to that conclusion after a continuous and relentless search after Truth which began nearly fifty years ago. I then found that the nearest approach to Truth was love. But I also found that love has many meanings in the English language at least and that human love in the sense of passion could become degrading also. I found, too, that love in the sense of never found a double meaning in connection with truth and not even the atheists had demurred to the necessity or power of truth. But in their passion for discovering truth the atheists have not hesitated to deny the very existence of God—from their own point of view rightly. And it was because of this reasoning that I saw that rather than say God is Truth I should say Truth is God. I recall the name of Charles Bradlaugh who delighted to call himself an atheist, but knowing as I do something of, I would never regard him as an atheist. I would call him a God-fearing man though I know he would reject the claim. His face would redden if I would say, "Mr. Bradlaugh, you are a truth-fearing man and not a God-fearing man." I would automatically disarm his criticism by saying that Truth is God, as I have disarmed the criticism of many a young man. Add to this the difficulty that millions have taken the name of God and in His name committed nameless atrocities. Not that scientists very often do not commit cruelties in the name of truth. I know how in the name of truth and science inhuman cruelties are perpetrated on animals when men perform vivisection. There are thus a number of difficulties in the way, no matter how you describe God. But the human mind is a limited thing and you have to labour under limitations when you think of a being or entity who is beyond the power of man to grasp. And than we have another thing in Hindu philosophy, viz. God alone is and nothing else exists, and the same truth you find emphasized and exemplified in the kalema of Islam. There you find it clearly stated that God alone is and nothing else exists. In fact the Sanskrit word for Truth is a word which literally means that which exists—*Sat.* For these and several other reasons that I can give you I have come to the conclusion that the definition—Truth is God—gives me the greatest satisfaction. And when you want to find Truth as God the only inevitable means is Love, i.e., nonviolence, and since I believe that ultimately means and end are convertible terms, I should not hesitate to say that God is Love.

5. [What is truth?] A difficult question, but I have solved it for myself by saying that it is what the voice within tells you. How, then, you ask, different people think of different and contrary truths? Well, seeing that the human mind works through innumerable media and that the evolution of the human mind is not the same for all, it follows that what may be truth for one may be untruth for another, and hence those who have made experiment have come to the conclusion that there are certain conditions to be observed in making those experiments. Just as for conduction scientific experiments there is an indispensable scientific course of instruction, in the same way strict preliminary discipline is necessary to qualify a person to make experiments in the spiritual realm. Everyone should, therefore, realize

his limitations before he speaks of his inner voice. Therefore, we have the belief based upon experience, that those who would make individual search after truth as God, must go through several vows, as for instance, the vow of truth, the vow of Brahmacharya (purity)—for you can not possibly divide your love for Truth and God with anything else—the vow of nonviolence, of poverty and non-possession. Unless you impose on yourselves the five vows, may not embark on the experiment at all. There are several other conditions prescribed, but I must not take you through all of them. Suffice it to say that who have made these experiments know that it is not proper for everyone to claim to hear the voice of conscience and it is because we have at the present moment everyone claiming the right of conscience without going through any discipline whatsoever that there is so much untruth being delivered to a bewildered world. All that I can in true humility present to you is that truth is not to be found by anybody who has not got an abundant sense of humility. If you would swim on the bosom of the ocean of Truth you must reduce yourselves to a zero. Further then this I cannot go along this fascinating path.

6. I do not regard God as a person. Truth for me is God, and God's Law and God are not different things or facts, in the sense that an earthly king and his law are different. Because God is an Idea, Law Himself. Therefore, it is impossible to conceive God as breaking the Law, He therefore, does not rule our actions and withdraw Himself. When we say He rules our actions, we are simply using human language and we try to limit Him. Otherwise, He and His Law abide everywhere and govern everything. Therefore, I do not think that He answers in every detail every request of ours, but there is no doubt that He rules our action. And I literally believe that not a blade of grass grows or moves without His will. The free will we enjoy is less than that of a passenger on a crowded deck.

7. I [feel a sense of communion with God]. I do not feel cramped as I would on a boat full of passengers. Although I know that my freedom is less than that of a passenger, I appreciate that freedom as I have imbibed through and through the central teaching of the Gita that man is the maker of his own destiny in the sense that he has freedom of choice as to the manner in which he uses that freedom. But he is no controller of results. The moment he thinks he is, he comes to grief.

8. Man was supposed to be the maker of his own destiny. It is partly true. He can make his destiny only in so far as he is allowed by the Great Power which overrides all our intentions, all our plans and carries out His Own plans.

9. I call that Great Power not by the name of Allah, not by the name of Khuda or God but by the name of Truth. For me, Truth is God and Truth overrides all our plans. The whole truth is only embodied within the heart of that Great Power—Truth. I was taught from my early days to regard Truth as unapproachable—something that you cannot reach. A great Englishman taught me to believe that God is unknowable. He is Knowable to the extent that our limited intellect allows.

10. Truth is by nature self-evident. As soon as you remove the cobwebs of ignorance that surround it, it shines clear.

11. Every expression of truth has in it the seeds of propagation, even as the sun cannot hide its light.

12. Life is a very complex thing, and truth and nonviolence present problems, which often defy analysis and judgment. One discovers truth and the method of applying the only legitimate means of vindicating it, i.e., *Satyagraha* or soul-force, by patient endeavour and silent prayer. I can only

assure friends that I spare no pains to grope to my way to the right, and that humble but constant endeavour and silent prayer are always my two trusty companions along the weary but beautiful path that all seekers must tread.

13. You cannot realize the wider consciousness, unless you subordinate completely reason and intellect, and the body, too.

14. It is unnecessary to believe in an extra mundane Power called God in order to sustain our faith in ahimsa. But God is not a Power residing in the clouds. God is an unseen Power residing within us and nearer to us than finger-nails to the flesh. There are many powers lying hidden within us and we find this Supreme Power if we make diligent search with the fixed determination to find Him. One such way of ahimsa. It is so very necessary because God is in every one of us and, therefore, we have to identify ourselves with every human being without exception. This is called cohesion or attraction in scientific language. In the popular language it is called love. In the popular language it is called love. It binds us to one another and to God. Ahimsa and love are one and the same thing. I hope this is all clear to you.

15. I am but a poor struggling soul yearning to be wholly good—wholly truthful and wholly non-violent in thought, word and deed; but ever failing to reach the ideal which I know to be true. It is a painful climb, but the pain of it is a positive pleasure to me. Each step upward makes me feel stronger and fit for the next.

16. But I know that I have still before me a difficult path to traverse. I must reduce myself to zero. So long as one does not of his own free will put himself last among his fellow creatures, there is no salvation for him. Ahimsa is the farthest limit of humility.

17. I am impatient to realize the presence of my Maker, Who to me embodies Truth and in the early part of my career I discovered that if I was to realize Truth, I must obey, even at the cost of my life, the law of Love.

18. I have but shadowed forth my intense longing to lose myself in the Eternal and become merely a lump of clay in the Potter's divine hands so that my service may become more certain because uninterrupted by the baser self in me.

19. God as Truth has been for me a treasure beyond price; may He be so to every one of us.

20. Devotion to this Truth is the sole justification for our existence.

21. But He is no God who merely satisfies the intellect, if He ever does. God to be God must rule the heart and transform it. He must express Himself in every the smallest act of His votary. This can only be done through a definite realization more real than the five senses can ever produce. Sense perceptions can be, often are false and deceptive, however real they may appear to us. Where there is realization outside the senses it is infallible. It is proved not by extraneous evidence but in the transformed conduct and character of those who have felt the real presence of God within. Such testimony is to be found in the experiences of an unbroken line of prophets and sages in all countries and climes. To reject this evidence is to deny oneself.

22. But it is impossible for us to realize perfect Truth so long as we are imprisoned in this mortal frame. We can only visualize it in our imprisoned in this mortal frame. We can only visualize it in our imagination. We cannot, through the instrumentality of this ephemeral body, see face to face Truth which is eternal. That is why in the last resort one must depend on faith.

23. No one can attain perfection while he is in the body for the simple reason that the ideal state is impossible so long as one has not completely overcome his ego, and ego cannot be wholly got rid of so long as one is tied down by the shackles of the flesh.

24. Man will ever remain imperfect, and it will always be his part to try to be perfect. So that perfection in love or non-possession will remain an unattainable ideal as long as we are alive but towards which we must ceaselessly strive.

25. Our existence as embodied being is purely momentary; what are a hundred years in eternity? But if we shatter the chains of egotism, and melt into the ocean of humanity, we share its dignity. To feel that we are something is to set up a barrier between God and ourselves; to cease feeling that we are something is become one with God. A drop in the ocean partakes of the greatness of its parent, although it is unconscious of it. But it is dried up as soon as it enters upon an existence independent of the ocean. We do not exaggerate, when we say that life is a mere bubble.

26. A life of service must be one of humility. He, who could sacrifice his life for others, has hardly time to reserve for himself a place in the sun. Inertia must not be mistaken for humility, as it has been in Hinduism. True humility means most strenuous and constant endeavour entirely directed towards the service of humanity. God is continuously in action without resting for a single moment. If we would serve Him or become one with Him, our activity must be as unwearied as His. There may be momentary rest in store for the drop which is separated from the ocean, but not for the drop in the ocean, which knows no rest. The same is the case with ourselves. As soon as we become one with the ocean in the shape of God, there is no more rest for us, nor indeed do we need rest any longer. Our very sleep is action.

For we sleep with thought of God, in our hearts. This restlessness constitutes true rest. This never-ceasing agitation holds the key to peace ineffable. This supreme state of total surrender is difficult to describe, but not beyond the bound of human experience. It has been attained by many dedicated souls, and may be attained by ourselves as well. This is the goal which we of the Satyagraha Ashram have set before ourselves; all our observances and activities are calculated to assist us in reaching it. We shall reach it some day all unawares if we have truth in us.

27. No niggardly acceptance of the inevitable will appear pleasing to God. It must be a thorough change of heart.

28. I must go with God as my only guide. He is a jealous Lord. He will allow no one to appear before Him in all one's weakness, empty-handed and in a spirit of full surrender, and then He enables you to stand before a whole world and protects you from harm.

29. I have no special revelation of God's will. My firm belief is that He reveals Himself daily to every human being but we shut our ears to 'the still small voice'. We shut our eyes to the Pillar of Fire in front of us. I realize His omnipresence.

30. I do not want to foresee the future, I am concerned with taking care of the present. God has given me no control over the moment following.

31. The impenetrable darkness that surrounds us is not a curse but a blessing. He has given us power to see only the step in front of us, and it should be enough if Heavenly light reveals that step to us. We can then sing with Newman, "One step enough for me." And we may be sure from our past experience that the next step will always be in view. In other words, the impenetrable darkness is nothing

so impenetrable as we imagine. But it seems impenetrable when, in our impatience, we want to look beyond that one step.

32. We are living in the midst of death. What is the value of "working for our own schemes" when they might be reduced to naught in the twinkling of an eye, or when we may equally swiftly and unawares be taken away from them? But we may feel strong as a rock, if we could truthfully say "we work for God and His schemes". Then nothing perishes. All perishing is them only what seems. Death and destruction have them, but only then no reality about tem. For death and destruction is then but a change. . . .

33. Prayer is the very soul and essence of religion, and there-fore, prayer must be the very core of the life of man, for no man can live without religion.

34. When a man is down, he prays to God to lift him up. . . .

35. Human effort must be there always. Those who are left behind must have help. Such reconstruction as is possible sill no doubt undertaken. All this and much more along the same line can never be a substitute for prayer.

36. But why pray at all? Does He stand in need of prayer to enable Him to do His duty?

37. No, God needs no reminder. He is within everyone. Nothing happens without His permission. Our prayer is a heart search. It is a reminder to ourselves that we are helpless without His support. No effort is complete without prayer,—without a definite recognition that the best human endeavour is of no effect if it has not God's blessing behind. Prayer is a call to humility. It is a call to self-Purification, to inward search.

38. I ask those who appreciate the necessity of inward purification to join in the prayer that we may read the purpose of God in such visitations, that they may humble us and prepare us to face our Maker whenever the call comes, and that we may be.

39. Prayer is not asking. It is a longing of the soul. It is daily admission of one's weakness. It is better in prayer to have a heart without words than words without a heart.

40. We are born to serve our fellowmen, and we cannot properly do so unless we are wide awake There is an eternal struggle raging in man's breast between the powers of darkness and of light, and he who has not the sheet-anchor of prayer to rely upon will be a victim to the powers of darkness. The man of prayer will be at peace with himself and with the whole world, the man who goes about the affairs of the world without a prayerful heart will be miserable and will make the world also miserable. Apart therefore from its bearing on man's condition after death, prayer has incalculable value for man in this world of the living. Prayer is the only means of bringing about orderliness and peace and repose in our daily acts. We inmates of the Ashram who came here in search of truth and for insistence on truth professed to believe in the efficacy of prayer, but had never up to now made it a matter of vital concern. We did not bestow on it the care that we did on other matters. I awoke from my slumbers one day and realizes that I had been woefully negligent of my duty in the matter. I have suggested measures of stern discipline and far from being any the worse, I hope we are the better for it. For it is so obvious. Take care of the vital thing and other things will take care of themselves. Rectify one angle of the square and the other angles will be automatically right.

41. It is easy enough to say, "I do not believe in God." For God permits all things to be said of Him with impunity. He looks at our acts. And any breach of His law carries with it, not its vindictive, but its purifying, compelling punishment.

42. God is the hardest taskmaster I have known on earth, and He tries you through and through. And when you find that your faith is failing or your body is failing you, and you are sinking, He comes to your assistance somehow or other and proves to you that you must not lose your faith and that He is always at your beck and call, but on His terms, not on your terms.

1700s British and French first come to India

1843 British establish a colony in the Natal province in South Africa

1850 Indians begin entering Natal, South Africa, in large numbers

1858 British take control of India as a British colony

1869 Mohandas Karamchand Gandhi is born on October 2 in Porbandar

1876 Gandhi's family moves to Rajkot

1882 Gandhi marries Kasturbai Makanji; British impose Salt Act

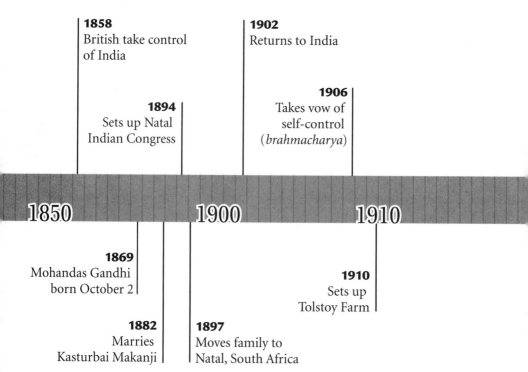

1858
British take control
of India

1902
Returns to India

1894
Sets up Natal
Indian Congress

1906
Takes vow of
self-control
(*brahmacharya*)

1850   1900   1910

1869
Mohandas Gandhi
born October 2

1910
Sets up
Tolstoy Farm

1882
Marries
Kasturbai Makanji

1897
Moves family to
Natal, South Africa

1885 Gandhi's father, Karamchand Gandhi, dies

1888 Gandhi studies one term at Samaldas College in Bhavnagar; son Harilal is born; Gandhi studies law in London; begins to simplify his life

1891 Gandhi's mother, Putlibai, dies; Gandhi passes bar exams; becomes a lawyer; returns to India; begins and quickly ends a law practice in Bombay; returns to Rajkot

1892 Son Manilal is born

1893 Works as clerk and translator for Indian ship trader in Durban, Natal, South Africa

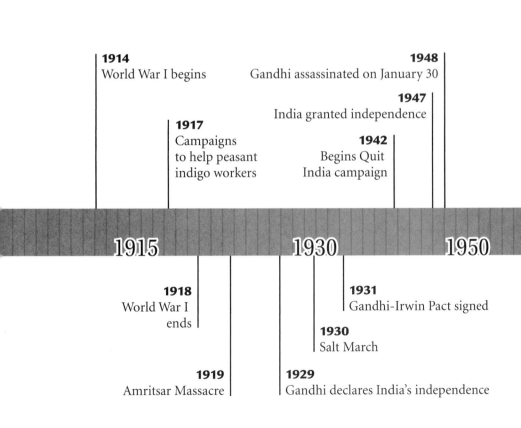

1914
World War I begins

1948
Gandhi assassinated on January 30

1947
India granted independence

1917
Campaigns
to help peasant
indigo workers

1942
Begins Quit
India campaign

1915

1930

1950

1918
World War I
ends

1931
Gandhi-Irwin Pact signed

1930
Salt March

1919
Amritsar Massacre

1929
Gandhi declares India's independence

CHRONOLOGY

1894 Gandhi sets up the Natal Indian Congress; his public-speaking skills, leadership, and confidence grow; he becomes a symbol for defending rights of minorities

1896 Writes *The Green Pamphlet*

1897 Gandhi moves his family to Natal, South Africa; Natal legislature passes law giving equal voting rights to Indians as well as whites; Gandhi's son Ramdas is born

1899–1902 British defeat Boer settlers in four-year war; Gandhi runs Indian ambulance corps during Battle at Spion Kop

1900 Gandhi's son Devadas born

1902 Gandhi and his family return to India; Gandhi travels across India; witnesses discrimination against Untouchables by the castes; opens law office in Johannesburg, South Africa; aids poorest Indians

1904 Publishes *Indian Opinion;* sets up Phoenix Settlement in Natal

1906 Gandhi runs Indian ambulance corps, aiding the Zulus rebelling against British; takes ancient Hindu vow of self-control *(brahmacharya)*

1907 Asiatic Registration Bill passes into law; Indians call it the "Black Act;" Gandhi is arrested and jailed for not registering and carrying required permit; Gandhi is imprisoned three times for protesting the permit law

1908 Writes pamphlet *Hind Swaraj ("Indian Home Rule")*

1910 Sets up Tolstoy Farm outside of Johannesburg

1913 New law voids Indian marriages; Gandhi leads followers in series of protest marches

1914 Indian Relief Bill passes; World War I begins

1915 Gandhi contracts pleurisy and returns to India; Indians begin calling Gandhi *Mahatma* (Great Soul); Gandhi resumes traveling across India, witnessing majority of Indians living in poverty; Gandhi establishes Satyagraha Ashram in Kochrab

1917 Gandhi and followers accept Untouchable family into Satyagraha Ashram; first uses satyagraha in India, aiding peasants working British indigo fields

1918 Gandhi helps textile workers in Amedabad strike against low wages; plague breaks out in Kochrab; Gandhi moves Satyagraha Ashram to site near Sabarmati Central Jail; fasts three days until mill owners give textile workers small wage increase; Kheda satyagraha campaign convinces British to exempt poorest Indians from crop taxes; Gandhi teaches satyagraha to Indians in Gujarat region; tries to recruit Indians to fight in World War I; war ends in November

1919 Protests Rowlatt Act; founds newspaper *Young India;* Amritsar Massacre takes place

1921 Rioting Indians kill twenty-two British police officers in Chauri Chaura; Gandhi fasts five days; is appointed chief executive of Indian National Congress

1922 Gandhi imprisoned for inciting rebellion (violating Rowlatt Act)

1924 Gandhi is released from prison early; Hindu-Muslim riots take place; Gandhi fasts for twenty-one days

CHRONOLOGY

1927 Indians write their own constitution, called Nehru Report

1929 Gandhi declares India's independence; Jawaharlal Nehru unveils new flag

1930 Gandhi leads 241-mile march to Arabian Sea; violates Salt Act to protest salt tax; British police begin mass arrests, including Gandhi and son Ramdas; Gandhi is sent to Yeravda Prison in Poona; Indian poet Sarojini Naidu leads demonstration at Dharasana Salt Works; Gandhi visits rural villagers, working to improve their living conditions throughout the 1930s

1931 Gandhi-Irwin Pact is signed but Second Round Table Conference fails

1932 Gandhi is arrested for civil disobedience and sent back to Yeravda Prison; ends six-day fast in prison when London cabinet approves Yeravda Pact

1933 Gandhi founds newspaper *Harijan*; six months later, he is released from Yeravda Prison; Gandhi and Kasturbai walk twelve thousand miles across India, speaking against discrimination against Harijans

1934 Gandhi escapes assassination attempt

1936 Gandhi begins living in Sevagram Ashram in central India

1939–1945 World War II takes place

1942 Gandhi begins Quit India campaign; imprisoned at Aga Khan Palace

1943 Violence erupts across India; Gandhi survives twenty-one-day fast

1944   Kasturbai Gandhi dies; Gandhi is released from Aga Khan Palace

1946–1948   Gandhi tries to stop violence across India and bring peace between Hindus and Muslims

1947   India is granted independence from Great Britain; Jawaharlal Nehru becomes prime minister; bloodshed continues between Hindus and Muslims; Gandhi ends one-week fast when groups agree to end violence

1948   Violence continues; Gandhi ends three-day fast when all Delhi leaders sign agreement to end violence; Hindu extremists attempt to assassinate Gandhi on January 20; on January 30, Hindu man shoots Gandhi three times in chest, killing him

NOTES

CHAPTER 1:
MARCH TO THE SEA

1. Homer A. Jack, ed., *The Gandhi Reader: A Source Book of his Life and Writings.* Bloomington: Indiana University Press, 1956, pp. 236–237.
2. William L. Shirer, *Gandhi: A Memoir.* New York: A Touchstone Book, Simon & Schuster, 1979, pp. 17–18.
3. Quotation available online at *http://www.gandhiserve.org/information/ photobiography/readmore.html.*

CHAPTER 2:
GROWING UP IN INDIA

4. Mohandas K. Gandhi, *An Autobiography: The Story of My Experiments with Truth.* Boston: Beacon Press, 1957, p. 3.
5. Ibid., p. 9.

CHAPTER 3:
LEAVING HOME
FOR COLLEGE

6. Mohandas K. Gandhi, *An Autobiography: The Story of My Experiments with Truth.* Boston: Beacon Press, 1957, p. 36.
7. Ibid., p. 40.

CHAPTER 4:
LIVING IN SOUTH AFRICA

8. Mohandas K. Gandhi, *An Autobiography: The Story of My Experiments with Truth.* Boston: Beacon Press, 1957, p. 108.
9. Ibid., p. 117.
10. Ibid., p. 139.
11. Ibid., p. 192.
12. Ibid., p. 195.

CHAPTER 5: SATYAGRAHA

13. Mohandas K. Gandhi, *An Autobiography: The Story of My Experiments with Truth.* Boston: Beacon Press, 1957, p. 220.
14. Ibid., p. 248.
15. Quotation available online at *http://www.nalanda.nitc.ac.in/resources/ english/etext-project/Biography/gandhi/ part4.chapter24.html.*

16. Mohandas K. Gandhi, *Ashram Observances in Action,* trans. Gujarati by Valji Govindji Desai. Ahmedabad: Navajivan Publishing House, 1955, p. 112.
17. Ibid., pp. 111–112.
18. Homer A. Jack, ed., *The Gandhi Reader: A Source Book of his Life and Writings.* Bloomington: Indiana University Press, 1956, p. 138.
19. Louis Fischer, *The Life of Mahatma Gandhi.* New York: Harper, 1950, pp. 75–76.
20. Judith M. Brown, *Gandhi: Prisoner of Hope.* New Haven and London: Yale University Press, 1989, p. 43.

CHAPTER 6:
RETURNING TO INDIA

21. Mohandas K. Gandhi, *An Autobiography: The Story of My Experiments with Truth.* Boston: Beacon Press, 1957, p. 350.
22. Mohandas K. Gandhi, *Ashram Observances in Action,* trans. Gujarati by Valji Govindji Desai. Ahmedabad: Navajivan Publishing House, 1955, p. 3.
23. Gandhi, *An Autobiography: The Story of My Experiments with Truth,* p. 395.
24. Ibid., p. 397.
25. Ibid., p. 412.
26. Homer A. Jack, ed., *The Gandhi Reader: A Source Book of his Life and Writings.* Bloomington: Indiana University Press, 1956, p. 158.
27. Gandhi, *An Autobiography: The Story of My Experiments with Truth,* p. 428.
28. Ibid., p. 429.
29. Ibid., pp. 431–432.

CHAPTER 7:
MOVING TOWARD SWARAJ

30. Homer A. Jack, ed., *The Gandhi Reader: A Source Book of his Life and Writings.* Bloomington: Indiana University Press, 1956, p. 183.
31. William L. Shirer, *Gandhi: A Memoir.* New York: A Touchstone Book, Simon & Schuster, 1979, p. 34.
32. Ibid., p. 31.
33. Judith M. Brown, *Gandhi: Prisoner of Hope.* New Haven and London: Yale University Press, 1989, p. 188.

34. Mohandas K. Gandhi, *An Autobiography: The Story of My Experiments with Truth.* Boston: Beacon Press, 1957, p. 278.
35. Martin Green, *Gandhi: Voice of a New Age Revolution.* New York: The Continuum Publishing Company, 1993, p. 71.
36. Brown, p. 218.
37. Dennis Dalton, *Mahatma Gandhi: Nonviolent Power in Action.* New York: Columbia University Press, 1993, p. 100.
38. Shirer, p. 94.
39. Ibid.
40. Jack, p. 243.
41. Ibid., p. 241.

CHAPTER 8:
CONTINUED UNREST

42. Homer A. Jack, ed., *The Gandhi Reader: A Source Book of his Life and Writings.* Bloomington: Indiana University Press, 1956, p. 249.
43. Ibid., p. 253.
44. Ibid., p. 162.
45. Ibid., p. 296.
46. William L. Shirer, *Gandhi: A Memoir.* New York: A Touchstone Book, Simon & Schuster, 1979, p. 210.
47. Jack, p. 105.
48. Ibid., p. 337.
49. Ibid., p. 317.
50. Shirer, p. 211.
51. Ibid., p. 212.
52. Ibid., p. 213.

CHAPTER 9:
INDEPENDENCE AT LAST

53. Homer A. Jack, ed., *The Gandhi Reader: A Source Book of his Life and Writings.* Bloomington: Indiana University Press, 1956, pp. 413–414.
54. Judith M. Brown, *Gandhi: Prisoner of Hope.* New Haven and London: Yale University Press, 1989, p. 343.
55. Jack, p. 436.
56. William L. Shirer, *Gandhi: A Memoir.* New York: A Touchstone Book, Simon & Schuster, 1979, p. 221.
57. Ibid.
58. Ibid., p. 219.
59. Jack, p. 445.

CHAPTER 10:
NEVER FORGOTTEN

60. M. J. Akbar, *Nehru: The Making of India.* New York: Viking Penguin Inc., 1988, p. 433.
61. Dennis Dalton, *Mahatma Gandhi: Nonviolent Power in Action.* New York: Columbia University Press, 1993, p. 167.
62. Ibid., p. 182.
63. Nelson Mandela, Speech by President Mandela at the conferral of the freedom of Pietermaritzburg on Mahatma Gandhi, April 25, 1997. Available online at *http://www.mkgandhi.org/articles/speechnm.htm.*
64. Dalton, p. 66.
65. William L. Shirer, *Gandhi: A Memoir.* New York: A Touchstone Book, Simon & Schuster, 1979, p. 227.
66. Ibid.
67. Mohandas K. Gandhi, *An Autobiography: The Story of My Experiments with Truth.* Boston: Beacon Press, 1957, p. 504.

GLOSSARY

ahimsa—Nonviolence

ashram—Community of men of religion

bapu—Affectionate name for Gandhi, meaning "father"

Bhagavad Gita (Song of the Lord)—Sacred Hindu poem

Brahma—The Hindu Creator god

brahmacharya—Hindu vow of self-control

Brahmins—Highest Hindu caste (priests)

charkha—Spinning wheel

dhoti—A kind of loincloth, similar to shorts

diwan—Chief administrator

Harijans—Translated to mean "Children of God;" name that Gandhi used to replace "Untouchables"

hartal—Strike

Hind Swaraj (*"Indian Home Rule"*)—Pamphlet written by Gandhi and published in 1909

khadi—Coarse, hand-woven material

Krishna—Incarnation of Vishnu

Kshatriyas—Second-highest Hindu caste (princes and soldiers)

Mahatma—Great Soul

Ramanama—Hindu god

sadagraha—Firmness in a good cause

Sanskrit—Ancient Hindu language

Saptapadi—Hindu wedding custom

sari—Dress made of a long piece of material that is draped around a woman's body to make a long skirt and a covering for the upper body

satyagraha (*satya*)—Name given to Gandhi's system of nonviolent resistance; literally meaning "truth force" or "love force"

satyagrahi—One who practices satyagraha

Shaivism—Major Hindu sect whose members are devoted to Shiva

Shaktism—Major Hindu sect whose members worship Shakti

sheth—Headman of the community

Shiva—The Hindu Destroyer god

Shudras—Fourth-ranking Hindu caste (laborers and peasants)

swaraj—Self-rule

Vaishnavism—Major Hindu sect whose members are devoted to Vishnu

Vaishyas—Third-ranking Hindu caste (merchants and farmers)

Vishnu—The Hindu Preserver god

BIBLIOGRAPHY

BOOKS

Akbar, M.J. *Nehru: The Making of India.* Viking Penguin, Inc., 1988.

Attenborough, Richard. *In Search of Gandhi.* New Century Publishers, Inc., 1982.

Brown, Judith M. *Gandhi: Prisoner of Hope.* Yale University Press, 1989.

Dalton, Dennis. *Mahatma Gandhi: Nonviolent Power in Action.* Columbia University Press, 1993.

Erikson, Erik H. *Life History and the Historical Moment.* W.W. Norton & Company, Inc., 1975.

Fischer, Louis. *The Life of Mahatma Gandhi.* Harper, 1950.

Fishlock, Trevor. *Gandhi's Children: A Vivid Account of India Today.* Universe Books, 1983.

Gandhi, Mohandas K. *An Autobiography: The Story of My Experiments with Truth.* Beacon Press, 1957.

———. *Ashram Observances in Action,* trans. Gujarati by Valji Govindji Desai. Navajivan Publishing House, 1955.

Gardner, Howard. *Extraordinary Minds.* BasicBooks, 1997.

Green, Martin. *Gandhi: Voice of a New Age Revolution.* The Continuum Publishing Company, 1993.

Jack, Homer A., ed. *The Gandhi Reader: A Source Book of his Life and Writings.* Indiana University Press, 1956.

Nanda, B.R. *Mahatma Gandhi: A Biography.* Oxford University Press, 1992.

Power, Paul F., ed. *The Meanings of Gandhi.* Hawaii University Press of Hawaii, 1971.

Shirer, William L. *Gandhi: A Memoir.* A Touchstone Book, Simon & Schuster, 1979.

Smith, Huston. *The World's Religions: Our Great Wisdom Traditions.* Harper San Francisco, 1991.

WEBSITES

Comprehensive Site by Gandhian Institute Bombay Sarvodaya Mandal
  www.mkgandhi.org

The Official Mahatma Gandhi eArchive & Reference Library
  www.mahatma.org.in

FURTHER READING

PRIMARY SOURCES

Gandhi, Mohandas K. *An Autobiography: The Story of My Experiments with Truth*. Beacon Press, 1957.

———. *The Bhagavad Gita According to Gandhi*, ed. John Strohmeier. Berkeley Hills Books, 2000.

———. *Book of Prayers*. Berkeley Hills Books, 1999.

———. *Gandhi: "Hind Swaraj" and Other Writings*, ed. Anthony J. Parel. Cambridge University Press, 1997.

———. *Gandhi's Health Guide*. Crossing Press, 2000.

———. *Mohandas Gandhi: Essential Writings*, ed. John Dear. Orbis Books, 2002.

———. *Non-violent Resistance*. Dover Publications, 2001.

Nehru, Jawaharlal. *Discovery of India*. Oxford Press, 1990.

SECONDARY SOURCES

Dalton, Dennis. *Mahatma Gandhi: Nonviolent Power in Action*. Columbia University Press, 1993.

Fischer, Louis. *Gandhi: His Life and Message for the World*. Signet, 1982.

Martin, Christopher. *Mohandas Gandhi*. Lerner Publishing Group, 2000.

Rodd Furbee, Mike, and Mary Rodd Furbee. *The Importance of Mohandas Gandhi*. Gale Group, 2000.

Severance, John B. *Gandhi: Great Soul*. Clarion Books, 1997.

Sherrow, Victoria. *Mohandas Gandhi: The Power of the Spirit*. The Millbrook Press, 1994.

Shields, Charles J. *Mohandas K. Gandhi: Overcoming Adversity*. Chelsea House Publishers, 2002.

Shirer, William L. *Gandhi: A Memoir*. A Touchstone Book, Simon & Schuster, 1979.

Wolpert, Stanley. *Gandhi's Passion: The Life and Legacy of Mahatma Gandhi*. Oxford University Press, 2001.

WEBSITES

Comprehensive Site by Gandhian Institute Bombay Sarvodaya Mandal

www.mkgandhi.org

A site devoted to providing information on Gandhi's life, work, and philosophy for students, researchers, and other interested people.

Mahatma Gandhi Learning Center

www.geocities.com/Athens/Olympus/2305/

Provides a detailed overview of Gandhi's life and philosophy.

Mahatma Gandhi Research and Media Service

www.gandhiserve.org/

Includes archival documents, photographs, links to relevant sites, and recordings of speeches made by Gandhi himself.

M. K. Gandhi Institute

www.gandhiinstitute.org/

A site devoted to promoting Gandhi's ideals of nonviolence in today's modern world.

National Gandhi Museum

www.gandhimuseum.org/

Contains exhibits relating to the life and work of Gandhi, along with information about visiting the actual museum, located in Rajghat, New Delhi, India.

The Official Mahatma Gandhi eArchive & Reference Library

www.mahatma.org.in

Contains archives of documents, photographs, and other materials relevant to Gandhi's life and career.

INDEX

INDEX

Muslims
   and Gandhi's death, 85-86
   Hindus versus, 58, 60-61, 78-83,
      85-86
   and independence, 78-81
   and Pakistan, 79-81

Naidu, Sarojini, 66, 74, 77
Natal Indian Congress, 31
Natal, South Africa, Gandhi in,
   24-31, 32-33, 39-40
Nazis, and World War II, 72-73
Nehru, Jawaharlal, 62, 63, 64, 74,
   81, 82, 85-86, 88
Nehru, Motilal, 62, 63
Nehru Report, 62-63
newspapers, Gandhi founding
   Harijan, 70, 72
   Indian Opinion, 39-40, 61
   Young India, 57, 60, 73
Noakhali, India, Muslim-Hindu
   riots in, 79-80
nonviolence. *See ahimsa;*
   satyagraha

Pakistan, 79-81
Parsi sari, 32
passive resistance. *See ahimsa;*
   satyagraha
Patel, Vallabhbhai, 66, 81, 82-83,
   85
peasants, and Gandhi's first
   satyagraha campaign, 51-52
Phoenix Settlement, 40, 43, 44,
   48, 49, 50, 61
Plea for Vegetarianism (Henry
   Stephens Salt), 20
pleurisy, Gandhi suffering from,
   47
Pongola, S.S., 31
Porbandar, India ("White City"),
   Gandhi's early years in,
   7-11

Quit India campaign, 74

Rajkot, India
   Gandhi's early years in, 11
   Gandhi's return to as lawyer,
      22
Ramanama, 10
Rambha (nurse), 10
Round Table Conference
   First, 67-68
   Second, 67, 68
Rowlatt Act, 55, 57-58, 60

Sabarmati Central Jail, and
   Satyagraha Ashram, 53
Sabarmati River, and Satyagraha
   Ashram, 50-51, 52-53
sadagraha, 41
Safari, S.S., 25
salt
   and Dharasana Salt Works
      demonstration, 66
   and Gandhi-Irwin Pact, 67
   and march to Arabian Sea, 2-5,
      63-64
Salt, Henry Stephens, 20
Samaldas College, 17
Sanskrit, 15
Santiniketan, 50
Saptapadi, 12
satyagraha (truth force or love
   force; civil disobedience), 74-75
   and Asiatic Registration Bill,
      42-43
   critics of, 88
   definition of, 41-42
   and Gandhi-Irwin Pact, 67
   Gandhi living by, 4-5, 48
   Gandhi's first use of aiding
      peasants in British indigo
      fields, 51-52
   and Martin Luther King, 87
   legacy of, 89

INDEX

ABOUT THE CONTRIBUTORS

ANNE M. TODD lives in Prior Lake, Minnesota, with her husband, Sean, and three sons, Spencer, William, and Henry. She received a Bachelor of Arts degree in English and American Indian Studies from the University of Minnesota. She has written a number of children's books, including biographies about American Indians and informative books about American history.

MARTIN E. MARTY is an ordained minister in the Evangelical Lutheran Church and the Fairfax M. Cone Distinguished Service Professor Emeritus at the University of Chicago Divinity School, where he taught for thirty-five years. Marty has served as president of the American Academy of Religion, the American Society of Church History, and the American Catholic Historical Association, and was also a member of two U.S. presidential commissions. He is currently Senior Regent at St. Olaf College in Northfield, Minnesota. Marty has written more than fifty books, including the three-volume *Modern American Religion* (University of Chicago Press). His book *Righteous Empire* was a recipient of the National Book Award.

DATE DUE
